The Asian Literature Bibliography Series

GUIDE TO JAPANESE PROSE

The Asian Literature Program
of the Asia Society

General Editor

Guide to

Japanese Prose

ALFRED H. MARKS
AND
BARRY D. BORT

G. K. HALL & CO.
70 LINCOLN STREET, BOSTON, MASS.
1975

Library of Congress Cataloging in Publication Data

Marks, Alfred H.
   Guide to Japanese prose.

   (The Asian literature bibliography series)
   Includes index.
   1. Japanese prose literature—Translations into
English—Bibliography.   2. English prose literature—
Translations from Japanese—Bibliography.   I. Bort,
Barry D., joint author.   II. Title.   III. Series.
Z3308.L5M37   016.8956'3'008   74-20608
ISBN 0-8161-1110-3

MANUFACTURED IN THE UNITED STATES OF AMERICA

To
Sara Narvaez

CONTENTS

FOREWORD

This annotated bibliography series on Asian literature was initiated in response to the needs of the nonspecialist. In each volume, a general introduction to the literature under examination precedes the annotations which provide summaries and evaluations to selected works. It is hoped that these guides will aid educators and students of Asian literature as well as those in disciplines other than literature—Asian heritage studies, anthropology, history, philosophy, the social sciences —who wish to take advantage of translated literature as a rich source of material for their studies. Books that are not available in libraries may be ordered through the publishers or through such specialized bookstores as Paragon Book Gallery, New York, Hutchins Oriental Books, California, or The Cellar Book Shop, Michigan.

Naturally, each author has his own criteria for the way the material in his guide is selected, presented, and judged. However, the intent of the author has been to indicate clearly and honestly the range and artistic merit of all the titles annotated and thereby guide the reader to those specific works that will satisfy his scholarly and aesthetic needs.

Arranged by topic and chronology, each guide covers the translated literature from the earliest times to today, but none pretend to be comprehensive. In most cases, works that are not recommended or have been superseded by better versions have been excluded. Omitted also are very specialized studies and inaccessible translations (thus excluding much of what has appeared in magazines and journals), and a number of translations too new to have been included in the guides. This increase in translation activities is a welcome sign. It points to a growing awareness of the importance of listening to Asian voices (rather than only to Western interpreters of Asia) and to the growing recognition of the place of Asian writings in the world literature and of the place of translators in the creative field. Hopefully, these guides will serve the reader who later turns to translations not annotated or discussed here.

1

A series of this scope required the involvement of a number of people. I would especially like to thank the authors who have prepared these guides and the many scholars who have acted as consultants throughout the preparation of each manuscript, offering invaluable suggestions and criticism. Acknowledgment is also due Junnko Tozaki Haverlick of the Asian Literature Program of The Asia Society under whose editorial guidance these guides were prepared.

BONNIE R. CROWN, Director
Asian Literature Program

The Asia Society

NOTE TO THE READER

The works annotated in this *Guide* are in two sections. "Pre-Meiji Literature" covers prose writing in Japan from the earliest time to 1867. The "Meiji Literature and After" section continues from 1868 to the present day. The works are arranged chronologically (by authors' birthdates within the modern section). General anthologies are arranged by date of publication following each section.

Most works in the *Guide* are referred to by their translated titles, except when the Japanese title is in common usage in English. Each entry is introduced by the title as used in the edition being reviewed, with the Japanese title romanized and in brackets. Boldface numbers given in parentheses for cross-reference indicate entry numbers, not page numbers.

In Japanese, the family name is always given first. All Japanese names in this volume follow the Japanese usage, with the exception of names given to fictional characters, which remain as they appear in translation.

Consonants in Japanese are pronounced approximately as in English, and vowels are pronounced approximately as in Italian. Certain *u* and *o* vowel sounds are longer than others. They have usually been represented in the text with macrons—as in *ō* and *ū*—primarily with authors, book titles, and important place-names. For Abe Kōbō's given name each *o* is held, without a break, twice as long as the *o* without the macron.

Accentuation of Japanese words is completely different from that of English. The safest method of dealing with Japanese words is to pronounce them in a flat monotone—not accented and with no variation in pitch, continuing through the last syllable.

INTRODUCTION

This introduction is not an outline history of Japanese literature; nor is it a history of Japanese prose. The first is too vast a subject for an introduction such as this; the second, still too vast, cannot be presented separately from the rest of Japanese literature. What follows, then, is an attempt to provide only as much information about Japanese literature in general and Japanese prose in particular as is necessary to place the works reviewed in a historical context.

The record of Japanese literature and Japanese prose begins early in the eighth century with the compiling of the *Kojiki* (no. 1) in 712, and the *Nihongi* (no. 2) in 720. The *Kojiki* was ordered by the Emperor Temmu, who reigned from 673 to 686, and the *Nihongi* (usually referred to by the Japanese as the *Nihon Shoki*) is commonly associated with the Empress Jitō and evinces a wish to show the nation off as historically the peer of the dazzling Han and T'ang dynasties of neighboring China.[1] Both books give evidence of a spoken literature stretching many centuries into the past. The *Nihongi* is written entirely in Chinese except for the poems and names, in which the Japanese is written in Chinese characters used only for their phonetic value. The *Kojiki* is written partly in Chinese and partly in Japanese, with the Japanese passages also expressed in phonetic Chinese.

Court sponsorship was not directly responsible for the next important publication of Japanese literature, the poetic anthology called the *Manyōshū* ("Collection for Ten Thousand Generations," or "Collection of Ten Thousand Leaves") published about A.D. 759. It was brought out by a group of courtiers, not all known to us, in twenty scrolls containing a total of 4,516 poems, some composed as early as the Nintoku era (before A.D. 399) and others in the current Tempyō-hōji era (ca. 757). The *Manyōshū*, like the poems of the *Nihongi*, was written in Chinese characters employed phonetically. Subsequent anthol-

1. Cf. Introductions to *Nihongi* and *Kojiki* (see nos. 1 and 2) and G. B. Sansom, *Japan, A Short Cultural History* (New York, D. Appleton-Century, 1943), pp. 20–29.

ogies, although using the *Manyōshū* as a model, were commissioned directly by the throne and included twenty-one separate projects, beginning with the *Collection of Ancient and Modern Times (Kokinshū)* of A.D. 905 and ending with the work that styled itself as the sequel of that first anthology, the *New Collection of Ancient and Modern Times Continued (Shinzokukokinshū)* of the year 1439.[2]

The prose of these centuries during which the imperial anthologies were published has five principal features: (1) developing use of Japanese due to gradual standardization of the Chinese characters used to represent Japanese syllables and the modification of those characters into graphs comparable in their simplicity with English script;[3] (2) frequent use of poems and poetic passages; (3) continuing concern with tales and themes from the oral tradition predating written literature; (4) the recurrence of the *monogatari*, or romance, and *nikki*, or diary, each in various forms; and (5) the strength and importance of women authors.[4] The *monogatari* and *nikki* forms require careful examination at the start. In general, however, rather than treat each feature separately, we will proceed alternately by genre and chronology through the great Nara (710–794) and Heian (794–1185) eras. The five features that mark the prose fiction of these centuries will be apparent again and again in the discussion.

The *monogatari*—literally, "the telling of things"—is to Japanese literature what the courtly love tradition out of the southern French province of Languedoc is to European literature. There are several kinds of *monogatari*, representing quite different genres, just as there are many different kinds of tales and romances in the West.

The first *monogatari* form requiring discussion is the *uta-monogatari*, or "poem-tale," a narrative studded with poems produced by the characters as commentary, repartee, correspondence, and even ritual as the story moves along. The

2. See Robert Brower and Earl Miner, *Japanese Court Poetry* (Stanford: Stanford University Press, 1961), pp. 481–487.

3. See Roy Andrew Miller, *The Japanese Language* (Chicago: Chicago University Press, 1967).

4. See Donald Keene, "Feminine Sensibility in the Heian Era," in *Landscapes and Portraits* (Tokyo: Kodansha, 1971).

best known example of this form is *The Tales of Ise (Ise Monogatari)*, which appeared late in the ninth century and was further embellished in the tenth. It is a somewhat disjointed history of the life of the poet, Ariwara no Narihira (825–880), and contains many of his poems as well as some of his prose works. *The Tales of Ise* will not be discussed in this *Guide* since it and the *uta-monogatari* form seem more properly poetry than prose.

But in the *tsukuri-monogatari*, or "fictional tale," the prose heavily outweighs the poetry in bulk and importance. This form is best represented by *The Tale of Genji* (no. 5), written about A.D. 1000 by Murasaki Shikibu, a lady of the court. Japan's outstanding literary work and one of the world's great artistic masterpieces, it contains almost eight hundred poems in Arthur Waley's slightly abridged translation, still not an overwhelming number in the 1,100 small-type pages of the edition available to readers of English.

Third is the group of *monogatari* usually identified with what is called the *setsuwa* tradition. Classification of this group is extremely complex, but the works in this category are usually collections of short tales, often of folk origin, sometimes secular, frequently Buddhist or Confucian, and frequently written in Chinese or heavily dependent on Chinese sources.[5] Two of the best-known *monogatari* of this group are the *Uji Shūi Monogatari* (no. 12) and *Konjaku Monogatari* (no. 11).

The fourth group of *monogatari* is the *gunki monogatari*, or "war tales," which did not emerge strongly in Japan until the courtly Heian era ended amidst military power struggles and feuds. The most celebrated work in this group is the *Heike Monogatari* (no. 9)—source of many of the plots which have long characterized Japanese fiction and drama. The tale is concerned with the last stages of the wars between the two imperial-guard families, the Hei or Taira, and the Gen or Minamoto, in which the prize was control of the royal family and hence the nation. When that war ended in 1185, the Heian period was over and the power of the imperial court secondary to that of the ruling warrior clan and its head, the *shōgun*, or mili-

5. For a full discussion of the tradition see D. E. Mills, *A Collection of Tales from Uji* (no. 12).

tary dictator. A fifth *monogatari* form, the *rekishi monogatari*, or "history tale," will be defined more fully when the war tale is discussed again in its chronological setting.

The *nikki*, or "diary" form, is narrated in the first person and tends to deal with real events, but it has certain points in common with the *monogatari* in its outlook and subject matter. Although it might be compared to the diary of Samuel Pepys, it is for the most part an account of the inner life of the writer (sometimes the persona the writer is assuming) and is preoccupied with the activities that the Japanese, particularly in the *monogatari*, have always seen as comprising the true milieux of literature: flower and moon viewing, poetry exchanges, music, dance, aesthetic conversation, calligraphy, and the passage of time.

The Tosa Diary (in no. **20**) of 935 provides an excellent beginning for a chronological discussion of the literature of the Heian period. It was written by one of the great literary masters of the time, Ki no Tsurayuki, editor of the first great imperial poetry anthology, the *Kokinshū*. He writes as if he were a lady returning by boat to the capital city after accompanying her husband on a tour of government service in one of the outlying districts, and presents in first person narration the incidents, the conversations, and the poetry of that voyage. For the first time in an important Japanese prose piece, the *kana* phonetic script is used. With *The Tosa Diary*, it became possible for Japanese court vernacular language to break away from Chinese in its written form. Perhaps it was in justification of his use of an orthography at that time thought not really worth a serious scholar's attention that Tsurayuki assumed the persona of a woman in the diary.

The Tosa Diary, heavily weighted with thirty-one-syllable poems, the *tanka*, has a subtle relationship with the travel diary of Matsuo Bashō, *The Narrow Road to the North* (nos. **23**, **24**) written over seven centuries later. A somewhat fictionalized account of a trip Bashō took in 1689, *The Narrow Road to the North* is studded not with *tanka* but with *haiku*, a form that came into vogue in the seventeenth century. The manifold permutations of the *nikki* form may be seen even later in the *shishōsetsu*, or "I-novels" of the twentieth century, as well as

in the great mass of novels related to them through which one
may observe the semi-public parading of autobiographical incidents and concerns of the author under thin, sometimes osten-
tatiously transparent disguise.

The Gossamer Years (no. **4**), written in the second part of the
tenth century, is the record of twenty very painful years in
the life of a Heian lady married to a high-ranking, philandering
husband. To Edward Seidensticker, its translator, the book represents "the first attempt in Japanese literature ... to capture
on paper, without evasion or idealization, the elements of a
real social situation" (p. 13). In the next century, *The Diary
of Murasaki Shikibu* (in no. **21**) was written by the author of
The Tale of Genji.

Slightly younger than Lady Murasaki was Lady Sarashina.
The dreamlike quality of her diary, often referred to as the
Sarashina Diary, is captured in the Ivan Morris translation, in
which it bears the title *As I Crossed a Bridge of Dreams* (no. **7**).
Professor Morris sees this work as, among other things, "one
of the first extant examples of the typically Japanese genre of
travel writing" (p. 17). The tradition of the diary as written
by a woman culminates in *The Izayoi Nikki* (in no. **26**) written
by the nun Abutsu less than a century after the end of the
Heian period. Like the *Sarashina Diary*, *The Izayoi Nikki* is important for its travel sections. Its translator, Edwin Reischauer,
in fact, feels that "it might be better classed as a travel account
or ... as a purely poetical work" (p. 14).

Varying slightly from the *nikki* was the *zuihitsu*, or miscellany,
of which the outstanding example is *The Pillow Book* (no. **6**),
written by the brilliant and witty Sei Shōnagon, a contemporary
of Lady Murasaki. The other great miscellany in Japanese literature is *Essays in Idleness* (no. **13**), by the monk Yoshida Kenkō
about 1330. Although the books are placed in the same genre,
the tremendous differences in the times, the situations, and
the philosophies of their authors make for a wide differentiation
in content and outlook. Each represents, in fact, a quintessential
view of the time from which it sprang.

Basic to the Heian period, however, is the fictional tale form,
which some see as developing from the short *Taketori Monogatari*

or *Tale of the Bamboo Cutter*,[6] which is believed to have been written in the middle of the ninth century.[7] This was followed by the *Utsubo Monogatari* (Tale of the Hollow Tree), and the *Ochikubo Monogatari* (no. 3). The great ripening of the form came about the year A.D. 1000 with the composition of *The Tale of Genji*, so important in Japanese culture and in world literature that one cannot accord it too many superlatives. It was followed later in the eleventh century by the *Tsutsumi Chūnagon Monogatari* (in no. 26), claimed by many to be the first book of short stories ever written.

All of these works show a growing mastery of prose fictional techniques, and of the written language employed to sustain them. Although both the *Ochikubo Monogatari* and the *Tsutsumi Chūnagon Monogatari* have been attributed to male as well as female authors, all attest to the high degree of aesthetic and literary sensibility of Heian womanhood and—as Donald Keene has shown—"the strength of the feminine influence in the arts of the period."[8]

In the years from 1185 to about 1600, the vital center of Japanese culture shifted from the imperial court, which possessed no effective military strength of its own, to the citadel of the feudal baron most powerful at the time. From 1185, the Minamoto clan, finally victorious over the Tairas, ruled in Kamakura, near present-day Tokyo, far from the city of Heian—now Kyoto—where the emperor reigned in splendid powerlessness with his retinue. Before thirty-five years had passed the Minamotos were given the same treatment they had given the emperor, and real power passed to the Hōjō clan, from whom Minamoto Yoritomo had taken his wife. The Hōjōs served as regents over puppet shōguns for another century, when they were removed from office not by an ambitious shōgun, nor by a royal regent running an effete emperor, but by an unusual incumbent emperor, Go-Daigo. Then, after a short restoration, Go-Daigo and his court were overthrown by Ashikaga Takauji, who installed a new line of emperors in spite

6. Translated by Donald Keene in *Monumenta Nipponica* 9, no.4 (1956).
7. Edwin O. Reischauer and Joseph K. Yamagiwa, trs., *Translations from Early Japanese Literature* (no. 26), p. 154.
8. Keene, "Feminine Sensibility in the Heian Era" (cited in note 4).

of Go-Daigo's objections and moved the new Ashikaga shogunate to the Muromachi section of Kyoto.

The Ashikagas ruled from Muromachi from 1336 to 1573. Then, after a period of shifting control by various competing military lords, Tokugawa Ieyasu, putatively a descendant of the Minamotos, became shōgun and moved the seat of government to Edo, later named Tokyo, where it remains to this day. The Tokugawas ruled from 1600 to 1867, when power was nominally restored to the Emperor Meiji, who then moved to the Tokyo of our time.

Through that period when overt military power kept a courtly oligarchy impotent, the war tales (gunki monogatari) naturally flourished. Sentimental, high flown, and extremely rhetorical, these works, as Joseph Yamagiwa says, "were intended, not to be read, but to be heard to the accompaniment of the biwa, or four-stringed lute, played by the biwa priests (biwa hōshi) who roamed the country and held their audiences in rapt attention as they chanted the fall of men in battle."[9] The period is still to the Japanese what the nineteenth century with its cowboys, Indian wars, and pioneer life is to the American. Many Americans have seen the Japanese film The Seven Samurai, and many more, as well as the Japanese themselves, know well the film The Magnificent Seven, the American Western based on it.

Chronological discussion of the gunki monogatari—not by nature a Heian genre—must be traced back to the Heian period and specifically to a more peaceful form, the rekishi monogatari, or "history tale," which is best represented in The Ōkagami (in no. 26), written somewhere about 1110, and in which the statesman Fujiwara Michinaga (966–1027) takes center stage. The history tale resembles the Kojiki and the Nihongi in content and outlook and, although represented in this Guide only by Ōkagami, it continued to be a vital genre until late in the eighteenth century.[10] Reischauer says of Ōkagami and the war tales:

9. In Japan, ed. Hugh Borton (Ithaca, N.Y.: Cornell University Press, 1950), p. 245.
10. For a full discussion of the genre see Reischauer and Yamagiwa, Translations, pp. 271–312.

... many literary predecessors lay behind the sudden flowering of the war tales in the early thirteenth century as the truest literary expression of the new social and political order. One predecessor was the historical tale, which had already become a popular literary form in the *Ōkagami* of the late eleventh or early twelfth century. It was a natural shift, consistent with the change in the spirit of the age, from romanticized historical narratives about the great court nobles, written in the spirit of the old court aristocracy, to romanticized accounts of the battles of the early feudal warriors, told from the point of view of the new military class.[11]

Hōgen Monogatari (no. **8**) and *Heiji Monogatari* (in no. **26**), written in the first half of the thirteenth century, are war tales that hearken back to the last decades of the Heian period and relate the story of the first great phases of the war between the Minamotos and the Tairas, from which the Taira clan emerged for a time victorious. *Heike Monogatari* (no. **9**) depicts the events which led to eventual victory for the Minamotos. *Taiheiki* (no. **10**), written a century later, deals primarily with the abortive effort of the Emperor Go-Daigo to effect a restoration of imperial power early in the fourteenth century. In the excellent introduction to her translation of that work, Helen Craig McCullough strikes the keynote for the historicity of the *Taiheiki* and some other works of the war-tale tradition by quoting from a ninth-century Italian biographer:

Where I have not found any history of any of these bishops, and have not been able by conversation with aged men, or inspection of the monuments, or from any other authentic source, to obtain information concerning them, in such a case, in order that there might not be a break in the series, I have composed the life myself with the help of God and the prayers of the brethren.[12]

The miscellany *Essays in Idleness*, which has been discussed earlier, and *An Account of My Hut* (in nos. **14**, **27**), another monk's diary written by Kamo no Chōmei in 1212, show a different side of Kamakura's history. As McCullough points out, "the society of fourteenth-century Japan ... was made up of three major elements, the Kyoto court, the great Buddhist

11. Ibid., p. 378.
12. Agnellus, Bishop of Ravenna, taken from G. C. Coulton, *Medieval Panorama*, (New York: Meridian Books, 1955), p. 439.

monasteries, and the provincial warriors" (p. xix). The monasteries frequently wielded great military power and figure in many of the war tales, but these two diaries show a gentler, more contemplative side of the monastic life against a happily muted background of murder and plunder. The books thus attest to the continuation of many of the delicate and civilized values of Heian times.

The 260-year span between 1336 and the beginning of the seventeenth century, when Tokugawa Ieyasu came to power and established the dynasty that would rule Japan until the Meiji era, was a period of continued and worsening political turmoil, but at the same time it was characterized by a flowering of the arts. Unfortunately for Japanese prose, however, many of the gentler forms of the *monogatari* and the *nikki* virtually disappeared, leaving primarily the war tale[13] and the history tale. Drama and poetry, especially the noh play and the *renga* or linked-verse form of poetry, developed in various exciting ways aided by monastic influences, principally in the growing intellectual domination of the Zen sect.

The dynasty of the Ashikaga shōguns collapsed about 1500. The resultant chaos lasted for about a century, and is usually called the *sengoku jidai*, or "period of warring states." It was gradually brought under control by three successive leaders: Oda Nobunaga, Toyotomi Hideyoshi, and Tokugawa Ieyasu. Nobunaga ruled from the fortress called Azuchi, in the Ōmi area near Kyoto, from 1568 until his assassination in 1582. His vassal Hideyoshi then set about securing his succession, which he accomplished in 1584, ruling from the palace named Momoyama until he died in 1598, when Tokugawa Ieyasu took power. The so-called Azuchi, Momoyama, and Edo periods of these three men each left their distinctive imprint on the arts of Japan.

The Edo period of Tokugawa Ieyasu is noted for its suppression of the samurai class and the rise to fairly conspicuous affluence of its merchant class. The noun *ukiyo*, or "floating world," best characterizes the Edo period, particularly in its first one hundred and fifty years. The term *ukiyoe*, or "floating world print," used at times to refer to all Japanese prints, is known to most beginning students of Japanese art.

13. See passage from the *Masukagami*, or "Mirror of Increase," in Donald Keene's *Anthology of Japanese Literature* (no. **27**), pp. 242–257.

It is with the genre called *ukiyozōshi*, or "tale of the floating world," that prose came back into Japanese literature in quality sufficient to attract translators now working in English. The form, as shown by G. W. Sargent (in no. **16**), developed out of the *kanazōshi*, works which were written for the rising bourgeoisie by members of the former samurai aristocracy. They were sometimes educational, frequently entertaining, and fell "into three categories: entertainments, practical guides, and Buddhist or Confucianist tracts" (p. xxvii). The *kanazōshi* enjoyed a vogue extending from the very beginning of the seventeenth century. *The Seventeen Injunctions of Shimai Sōshitsu* and *The Millionaire's Gospel*, both by anonymous authors, are related to the *kanazōshi* tradition, and thus are translated by Sargent in his edition of Saikaku's *ukiyozōshi*, *The Japanese Family Storehouse* (no. **16**).

Saikaku, one of the great masters of Japanese prose, alternates between austere, didactic moralizing and carefree, pagan lust in his tales. Their settings are the counting room, the middle-class home, the gay quarters of various cities, and the open road where travelers meet and sojourn at inns along the way. Saikaku's compact style and highly allusive imagery may be traced to his earlier success as a writer of *haikai*, the light form of the linked verse or *renga* from which the *haiku* form later developed.

Saikaku provides, one might say, a continental divide between the old aristocratic, courtly prose—part fiction, part essay, part diary—and the new bourgeois, townsman prose, exciting in content, heavily though often hypocritically didactic, and sometimes illustrated with drawings of great virtuosity. This new prose, like the *monogatari*, proliferated into many types and subtypes.

A new variation on the old diary, in which *haiku* instead of *tanka* were interspersed with prose, developed at about the same time. This is best illustrated in the writings of Bashō, most notably in *The Narrow Road to the North* (nos. **23, 24**). A nineteenth-century example of the form may be seen in Shiki's *The Verse Record of My Peonies* (in no. **20**).

The proliferating forms of bourgeois prose, frequently subsumed under the term *gesaku* or "light literature," included the *kanazōshi* and its *ukiyozōshi* variation espoused by Saikaku, and the romantic yet didactic "grass books" (kusazōshi), which were further classified into so-called "red books" (akahon) and "yellow covers" (kibyōshi), and many other types and subtypes. Most important of the gesaku forms was the "reading book" (yomihon), a didactic, chauvinist form of the historical novel. Its principal exponent was Takizawa Bakin, who in the early nineteenth century wrote over thirty full-length works, which inspired his principal biographer, Leon Zolbrod, to compare him to Sir Walter Scott. Zolbrod's statement of how the historical romance is employed in the hands of Bakin says much about the yomihon form:

The main action in Eight "Dogs," for example, treats events of 1441–84, but his mention of Kabuki, the puppet theater, firearms, and so on, indicates that Bakin was concerned with more than history. Customs prevailing in his own day are often ascribed to a bygone age. Among these are harakiri and highly dramatic (though artificial) conflicts between loyalty and filial piety. Such anachronisms were equally common in the theater, but Bakin used them to alert his readers that his aim was to write didactic romances, not accurate histories.[14]

Sometime between 1803 and 1810, a contemporary of Bakin, Jippensha Ikku, began publishing in installments a book named Tokaidōchū Hizakurige (no. 25), meaning approximately "Afoot on the Tōkaidō Road." It represented still another bourgeois tradition, that of the "funny book" (kokkeibon). It is the story of a trip along the Tōkaidō Road between Tokyo and Kyoto taken by two men whose names, Yajirōbei and Kitahachi, amuse Japanese readers as names like Huckleberry and Yogi amuse American readers. This book conveys the flavor of a less complex Japan with its simpler Tōkaidō Road, as depicted by Hiroshige and Hokusai, Ikku's contemporaries, in their great woodblock prints. That simpler Japan and the best of paperback works of light literature that characterized it would soon change drastically. Less than twenty-five years after the death of Ikku, less than a decade after the deaths of Bakin and Hokusai, and five years before that of Hiroshige, Commodore Perry sailed into Tokyo Bay.

14. Leon Zolbrod, Takizawa Bakin (New York: Twayne, 1967), p. 66. This book, incidentally, is an extremely valuable source of information on the literature of the late eighteenth and early nineteenth centuries.

In 1885 Tsubouchi Shōyō, a novelist and translator, published a book titled *The Essence of the Novel (Shōsetsu Shinzui)*, which sounded the death knell for many of the existing popular genres of Japanese prose and prepared the way for new genres that continue vigorously even today. Tsubouchi says of the literature of his time:

Moreover, since popular writers have no choice but to be devoid of self-respect and in all things slaves to public fancy and the lackeys of fashion, each one attempts to go to greater lengths than the last in pandering to the tastes of the time. They weave their brutal historical tales, string together their obscene romances and yield to every passing vogue.[15]

Influenced by Tsubouchi, Futabatei Shimei produced the novel *Ukigumo* (no. **30**) in 1889. Futabatei may have referred more than once to this statement by Tsubouchi:

The novel should be concerned with the emotions of men and the ways of the world. By emotions I mean passion and feeling. The seven emotions of man are joy, anger, grief, fear, love, hate, and desire. The talent of a true novelist lies in his ability to depict these emotions, to investigate them carefully—minutely, exhaustively, leaving little out —to make hypothetical, imaginary people move within the structure of his plot until we can see them as real people. Because the task of the novel is to reflect mankind, those which simply picture man's outer life should not be called novels. When they reach the point where they study the essence of mankind, then, for the first time, we will see a true novel.[16]

The ensuing discussion of Japanese literature in this Introduction will proceed almost entirely in accordance with the terms Tsubouchi Shōyō broached, terms which have points in common with the critical traditions of fiction then and still current in Europe and the West, but which in Japanese literature keep returning to the central problem Tsubouchi delineated: the novelist must go beyond picturing "man's outer life" and "study the essence of mankind" in all its subtle manifestations.

Tsubouchi's most important influence at first was on the

---

15. In Donald Keene, *Modern Japanese Literature* (no. **114**), p. 57.
16. Marleigh Grayer Ryan, *Japan's First Modern Novel: Ukigumo* (no. **30**), p. 52.

novelist's approach to his trade. As shown by Nakamura Mitsuo, in his *Modern Japanese Fiction*, the Japanese novelist before Tsubouchi maintained a perverse pride in his status as a writer of light literature.[17] The entire field seemed to be dominated by one Kanagaki Robun, known to readers of English only as the author of "The Beefeater"—a two-page snippet from his novel *Aguranabe* translated by Donald Keene in his *Modern Japanese Literature* (no. **114**). According to Nakamura, Kanagaki's influence was so strong that no author could hope for literary success unless he became Kanagaki's disciple. Tsubouchi did not lessen the tendency of Japanese literature to break down into schools dominated by one or two strong figures, and he did not put an end to light literature. But he did prepare the way for certain of the great literary figures emerging in his time to take up authorship as a serious profession, and for varying periods of time to depend on it entirely as their source of income without consulting Kanagaki Robun or his successor.

Four important writers of the Meiji period will be discussed here: Kunikida Doppo, Tayama Katai, Mori Ōgai, and Natsume Sōseki. The last two are acknowledged masters. Five of Kunikida's stories were recently published in translation in a special edition of *Monumenta Nipponica* (no. **45**), but neither he nor Tayama have had any full-length works translated into English, despite the fact that they are the principal figures in two important traditions in modern Japanese fiction—naturalism and the I-novel.

Kunikida's "Old Gen," translated by Jay Rubin in *Monumenta Nipponica*, contains a fascinating blend of Western styles. The exposition and complex narrational point of view are highly suggestive of the writing of Ambrose Bierce, in particular his story "The Boarded Window." It is conceivable that Doppo knew the Bierce story. "Old Gen" is also strikingly similar to Sherwood Anderson's "Death in the Woods." Anderson's story, for instance, is told in the first person, and it deals with fragments of the life of another person the narrator—seemingly Anderson himself—has become interested in and which lead him, "like music heard from far off" to learn more about that

17. Nakamura Mitsuo, *Modern Japanese Fiction* (Tokyo: Japan Cultural Society, 1968), p. 35.

person and eventually tell her story, with obvious assistance at crucial points from Anderson's fertile imagination. "Old Gen" also deals with a story partially told to a man called simply "the young teacher," to whom the story of Old Gen seems "something like a box, containing some mystery or some answer, which no one could open any longer." After a time the young teacher completes the story, also presumably from his own rich imagination.

Kunikida Doppo is noted for his part in the formulation of the basic ideas of Japanese naturalism, a movement Nakamura Mitsuo sees as having "incomparably great importance" in the novel of the Meiji and Taishō eras.[18] One who comes to the term *naturalism* as used in Japanese literature expecting to find what is meant by American or even French naturalism will be surprised. In the first place, Japanese naturalism avowedly possesses a heavy admixture of romanticism. Nakamura describes it in these words:

In France and other countries ... naturalism and the scientific thought were a reaction against Romanticism and its essence—liberation of human feelings. In Japan, however, one of the main features of naturalism was that it was one phase of Romanticism that later on served to perfect Romanticism.[19]

Kunikida's own words on the subject bring his naturalism, romantic as it may have been, into close touch with the words of Tsubouchi quoted earlier on the importance of using the novel to "study the essence of mankind ... minutely, exhaustively, leaving little out." In his work *Okamoto's Notebook* (*Okamoto no Techō*). Kunikida wrote:

My deepest desire is to wake out of sleep, to shake off my dreams, to look straight at this strange, boundless universe and life in this universe. To find my naked self in this strange universe. Not merely to know about strangeness. Not to know about death, but to stand in awe of the reality of death. Not to gain faith, but to feel the fearful reality of this universe as it is, to such an extent that I cannot even have a moment's peace of mind without believing.[20]

18. Ibid., p. 95.
19. Ibid., p. 102.
20. Ibid., p. 100.

In a nation long attracted to the diary, this concern with the inner reality of personal life—meaning often the author's own life—was bound to lead to the autobiographical novel. The first important representative of that form was the novel usually referred to in English as *The Quilts* (*Futon*) by Tayama Katai. The title might more accurately be translated "The Bed," since the *futon* in Japanese is the roll of bedding spread on the *tatami* floor for sleeping. The title also has erotic overtones, for it deals with an extramarital affair of the author. *The Quilts* is the first of three autobiographical or I-novels (*shishōsetsu*) by Katai, and is usually seen as marking the full onset of Japanese naturalism with its publication in 1907. The only work of Tayama Katai in English translation seems to be the story—not autobiographical—"One Soldier," included in Keene's *Modern Japanese Literature* (no. 114).

Mori Ōgai stood above the literary crosscurrents of his time. One reason for his detachment may have been his early training as a physician, which included four years of study in Germany. When he returned from Germany in 1888 he was equipped with ·a thorough education in German literature and ready to make his mark on the Japanese literary scene. Not long after his return he founded the literary magazine *Shigarami Zōshi*, and in 1890 published his first important prose piece, "Dancing Girl" (*Maihime*), which has not yet been translated. In the 1890s and the early 1900s he took positions opposed first to Tsubouchi Shōyō and later to naturalism.

The Ōgai works reviewed in this *Guide* emanate from the second great period of his literary activity which extended from 1909 until his death in 1922.[21] *The Wild Geese* (no. 28) was written in 1911, while Ōgai was still involved with modern-day novels, and *Sanshō-Daiyu* (no. 29) in 1915, after he had turned to historical novels. He closed his life with a string of biographies. The 1971 edition of his complete works runs to twenty-two volumes of literary criticism—strongly oriented toward German authors—novels, short stories, poems, plays, biographies, and more.

Natsume Sōseki also stands above his time, perhaps because

21. Ibid., pp. 16–17.

of his desire for solitude. Although his works reveal the influence of naturalism and the I-novel, and he was the great benefactor of the White Birch (Shirakaba) School (to be discussed below), even his protagonists reject community life in their lonely fictional worlds. Fortunately, Sōseki has received much attention from translators, and he is well represented in the *Guide*. But not enough can be said about the fine sensitivity he shows to the tugs and pulls of opposing Japanese and Western traditions in his time, and about the flashes of insight that occasionally brighten the gloomy lives of his characters. Beongcheon Yu says of Sōseki: "in diagnosing the tragic situation of modern Japanese intelligentsia, seeking in his tradition the inspiration for an acceptable ethos, and thereby suggesting the way it comes out of isolation into a wide world, Sōseki's art is also an art of hope, affirming the value of life, which tends to be lost in the frantic struggle between the old and the new."[22]

The Taishō era began in 1912, after the death of the Emperor Meiji, and the writers who established themselves in this period had new preoccupations. As usual with Japanese literary men, they grouped themselves into schools. There was the White Birch School, mentioned above, which developed around the magazine *Shirakaba* (White Birch) in 1910, and which is represented in the *Guide* primarily by Mushakōji Saneatsu, Shiga Naoya, and Arishima Takeo. Their effort was to escape the gloom of naturalism and present a brighter world in which the study of the human condition leads to admiration for the human ability to win out by conscious effort over the destructive forces of the universe. There was also the aesthetic school, represented in the *Guide* by Nagai Kafū and Tanizaki Junichirō. Kafū turned for his inspiration to old Tokyo—or the remnants of it—and the gay quarters, once the subject of so many *ukiyoe* prints. (See no. **47** for his classic *Geisha in Rivalry* and no. **48** for his excellent novella *The Sumida River*.)

Tanizaki Junichirō, whose works Americans came to know well before his death in 1965, began his work as a disciple of Nagai Kafū but soon surpassed his master. The recurring theme of his writings is the domination of woman over man

22. Beongcheon Yu, *Natsume Soseki* (New York: Twayne, 1969), p. 178.

and man's wish to be continuously debased and imposed upon.[23] This may be seen in the works in the *Guide*, particularly in his late *Diary of a Mad Old Man*, in "The Tale of Shunkin," and in *The Key* (nos. **56, 53, 55**).

This discussion of the Taishō era would not be complete without mention of Akutagawa Ryūnosuke and Dazai Osamu, whose works have in common the authors' and their protagonists' tragic quest for meaning in a meaningless, venal world. Both authors committed suicide. Akutagawa is best known to Western readers as the author of the story "In a Grove" (in no. **62**), on which the Kurosawa film *Rashōmon* was based, and the story "Kesa and Morito" (in Keene's *Modern Japanese Literature*, no. **114**) which, along with a play by Kikuchi Kan, was the basis of Kurosawa's *Gate of Hell*. Akutagawa's stories are highly varied in content and are frequently renditions of tales from Japan's feudal period rewritten under the influence of twentieth-century psychological insights. Dazai Osamu is noted for the decadence and unrelieved gloom of his novels, such as *The Setting Sun* (no. **87**) and *No Longer Human* (no. **88**). But, as Donald Keene has shown in his essay on Dazai in *Landscapes and Portraits*, there is a lighter side to this writer's work, even in what seems to be its gloomiest passages.

The Shōwa era, which began in 1926, is, of course, our own time. However, because of the repressive influence of Japanese militarism, Shōwa literature did not come into its own until the years after World War II. These years have marked the real emergence of Japanese literature among the world's literatures, primarily by way of translation first into English, followed by translation into various European languages. The dominant authors of this period, those best known in the West, are Tanizaki Junichirō, Mishima Yukio, and Kawabata Yasunari, who received the Nobel prize for literature in 1968. Kawabata's reputation in the West was based, at the time of his award, on two slim novels, *Snow Country* and *Thousand Cranes* (nos. **72, 73**). The first deals with the protracted dalliance of a Tokyo family man with a hot-springs geisha, and the second with the futile attempts of a young man to determine his own future apart from the influences of the mistresses and the tea-ceremony

---

23. See Keene's delightful essay on Tanizaki in *Landscapes and Portraits*. See note 4 above.

utensils of his father. Mishima, who is now undoubtedly the best known Japanese author in the world, has been more translated than any other Japanese author. His writings, apart from his headline-making suicide, have made his reputation and his future in translation secure.

The dominant note in the works of Mishima, Kawabata, and Tanizaki, in spite of differences in their subjects, has been the interaction between their lives and their works—the autobiographical quality of their fiction. Autobiographical criticism is a legitimate, serious avenue of endeavor in Japanese literature, as it has never been in Western literature. The Japanese preoccupation with the author's life as related to his literature, as has been discussed earlier, goes back to the earliest works in the vernacular language, to the partly fictional *The Tosa Diary*, and to the also partly fictional autobiography-poem cycle *The Tales of Ise*. Tsubouchi Shōyō, Tayama Katai, and the naturalists carried this preoccupation, permuted by many centuries of use and change, into the novel, thus giving the Japanese novel as it exists even today one of its most prominent distinguishing features. Perhaps Norman Mailer, with his autobiographical *Armies of the Night* and *St. George and the Godfather*, has profited from the Japanese example.

Although Tanizaki, Mishima, and Kawabata, Japan's three literary giants, are gone, the future of Japanese literature is promising. There are still Abe Kōbō, whose novels continue to be translated yearly in spite of the repetitiveness of his themes; Endō Shūsaku, whose Roman Catholic upbringing has brought him into strong sympathy with Western martyrs in Japan, even into World War II; Niwa Fumio, whose *The Buddha Tree* (no. 81) is perhaps the finest study of the life of a Buddhist priest at work with his congregation available to the Western reader; and Inoue Yasushi, a prolific writer more popular among contemporary Japanese readers than perhaps any author discussed thus far. And there will be others—good writers and great writers. Of this the long past of Japanese prose assures us.

ANNOTATED
BIBLIOGRAPHY

Pre-Meiji Literature (Beginnings to 1867)

1. *Kojiki*. Tr. by Donald L. Philippi. Tokyo: University of Tokyo Press, 1968. 655 pp.

The *Kojiki* was written, along with the *History of Japan* (*Nihon Shoki*, no. **2**), in response to efforts of the Japanese government to place the nation and its imperial house in an earthly and cosmogonic historical order like that of their contemporary model, T'ang China. The *Kojiki*, completed about A.D. 712, attempts to go back to the beginnings of the nation. The *History of Japan*, while it chronicles ancient matters too, is concerned with more recent events. Both works are important, as useful in Japanese song and story as the Judaic Pentateuch is in Western literatures.

The *Kojiki* is a collection of myths and old tales interwoven with putative events from the lives of historical personages, primarily emperors. They fall into two different cycles: one grouped around the sun goddess Ama-terasu-opo-mi-kami, worshiped by the court; the other around the divine culture-hero, Opo-kuni-nusi. The old tales, mixtures of poetry and prose, are filled with imperial intrigues, battles, couplings, childbirths, and genealogies.

This edition is a marvel of dedicated scholarship and sensitive literary judgment. It includes, besides full translation of all three books of the *Kojiki*, two sets of notes, an appendix giving romanized texts of the songs referred to in the text, a glossary of place names and personal names, and a full bibliography in English, with romanized Japanese and *kanji*.

The text is as readable as possible, considering the difficulties of hyphenated names, the bristling footnote reference numbers, and the Old Testament style. The original also was deliberately cast in archaic language.

2. *Nihongi* (or *Nihon Shoki*). Tr. by W. G. Aston. (1896). London: George Allen and Unwin, 1956. xx, 443 pp.

The *Nihongi* is commonly paired with the *Kojiki* (no. 1), which was completed eight years before it. Both works were compiled in response to the same set of politico-historical needs in the Japanese court in the seventh century A.D. Donald Philippi, translator of the *Kojiki*, advises that the two works be studied together.

The *Nihongi* (literally, "History of Japan") opens with two long books on "The Age of the Gods," a somewhat Sinified set of myths beginning with the separation of Heaven and Earth and the creation of divine beings between them, and continuing through the "over 1,792,470 years" until the reign of the Emperor Jimmu, Japan's first emperor. The twenty-eight books that follow treat the reigns of each of the emperors up to the Empress Jitō, who reigned from 686 to 697, the time that the *Nihongi* was being written. The mythological material slowly falls away as the books advance, until finally, through the last twenty or so reigns, fairly dependable historical reporting takes over. According to Donald Philippi, "the Nihon shoki is our main historical source for the post-Kenzō [A.D. 487] reigns . . . a contemporary history, as trustworthy and useful a work as the other, later official histories."

The Aston translation is one of the wonders of nineteenth-century scholarship, but it is clearly out of date now. The Philippi *Kojiki* contains glossaries, notes, and romanized proper names that now make Aston's *Nihongi* slightly more usable; however, it is hoped that a full translation will appear, one that will be as useful for our time as was Aston's for his.

3. *Ochikubo Monogatari or The Tale of the Lady Ochikubo*. Tr. by Wilfrid Whitehouse and Yanagisawa Eizō. (1934). London: Peter Owen, 1970. 287 pp.

This is an extremely interesting work, readable and exciting. Yet it is also rather trite—in fact, a Heian potboiler. It was written shortly before *The Tale of Genji* (no. 5) and *The Pillow Book* (no. 6), in the latter of which this tale is mentioned, and is of about the same period as *The Gossamer Years* (no. 4). The plot is well organized by formulas that still apply today: (1)

Boy meets girl, boy loses girl, boy gets girl. (2) Wicked step-mother (with four daughters of her own) gets her comeuppance. (3) The ugly duckling eventually brings joy and reward to her old father, who loved her all the time although powerless to do much for her. She almost succeeds in making even her hardhearted stepmother see the injustices she has been perpetrating all these years.

The translation reads well, although it does not have a contemporary polish, and suggests the tone of an old translation from Hans Christian Andersen or the brothers Grimm. The *tanka*, 31-syllable poems interspersed in typical *tsukuri-monogatari* style, are rendered somewhat lamely in five lines, totaling 31 syllables. There are useful yet unobtrusive footnotes and two appendices—one on the tale, its author, and its literary milieu, the other on court departments and ranks.

4. The Mother of Michitsuna. *The Gossamer Years* [Kagerō Nikki]. Tr. by Edward Seidensticker. Rutland, Vermont: Charles E. Tuttle Co., 1964. 209 pp.

Kagerō Nikki is an early document in the Heian tradition of elegant writings in poetry and prose by court ladies. It is described by Ivan Morris in *The World of the Shining Prince* (New York: Knopf, 1964, p. 313) as the "earliest extant diary by a woman."

It is a rather peevish record, although the lady is justifiably peevish. She is allied, by a tie that can technically be called "marriage," to a ruling statesman who is attempting to maintain alliances with a number of other women simultaneously. We are not told whether one of the lucky ladies is designated his "kita no kata" or formally announced spouse. That honor was evidently not bestowed upon the author of this diary, who is known to the world simply as the mother of one of the statesman's sons.

The result is a delicate document of a disastrous marital relationship. It is filled with *tanka*, mostly his and hers: his tender solicitations—seemingly tossed off as he walks away—and her petulant replies. This relationship endures for about twenty years.

This book won a Japanese award for translation in 1966. The translation is easy to read, marred only by frequent footnote references completed in the back of the book. This fault could have been greater, for the text is known for the variations in its source documents, and the language is notoriously difficult. The translator discusses the complexities of his task in a full and useful introduction.

5. Murasaki Shikibu. *The Tale of Genji* [Genji Monogatari]. Tr. by Arthur Waley. (Houghton Mifflin, n.d.). New York: Random House, Modern Library, 1960. 1,135 pp.

The fictional life of an ideal courtier, written about the year A.D. 1000, *The Tale of Genji* is the most important book in Japan's literature. The life of Prince Genji, and this book about him, have been depicted in song and story and imitated in real life since Lady Murasaki created *Genji Monogatari* for the amusement of the retinue of the long-lived Empress Akiko, with whom she served for over two decades in the early part of the eleventh century.

The first four parts of the book recount the life and loves of the prince: his birth to a favorite, though lowborn, concubine of the emperor; his search for the ideal woman, beautiful, witty, literary, passionate, yet patient; his political advancement, culminating—in spite of a period of exile—in the post of Grand Minister, with power greater than that of the emperor; and above all his preoccupation with the arts we now think of as traditionally Japanese—calligraphy, painting, poetry, landscape gardening, costume, perfumes, dance, and music (both instrumental and vocal).

The last two parts, which deal with Genji's world after his death, recount the courting by Genji's grandson, Niou, and Genji's putative son, Kaoru, of two sisters who live a short distance from the capital in an old mansion beside a rushing river in a place called Uji (a pun on the Japanese word for sadness). These last parts of the book have strength and maturity of construction that compensate for the absence of Genji himself.

The movement of the plot through the multitudinous and at times harrowing adventures of Genji and his successors is slowed by interior monologue, descriptions of court events, poetic exchanges, and seasonal shifts—painstakingly described along with the accompanying costume changes. Matters of taste and social and intellectual complications brought about by sexual desire are carefully analyzed at every opportunity by the principal characters or the intrusive author.

Central to the novel is the aesthetic attitude called in Japanese *mono no aware*, defined in *The World of the Shining Prince* by Ivan Morris as follows:

> its most characteristic use in *The Tale of Genji* is to suggest the pathos inherent in the beauty of the outer world, a beauty that is inexorably fated to disappear together with the observer. . . . The sensitive observer is moved to tears by the beauty of nature, or by its embodiment in art (the Emperor's reaction to Genji's dance will be recalled), not only because it is so impressive in itself, but because when confronted with such beauty he becomes more than ever conscious of the ephemeral nature of all that lives in this world of ours. [New York; Knopf, 1964, pp. 196–197]

The Tale of Genji must be treated, therefore, as a succession of episodes depicted within deep and exquisitely wrought aesthetic frames. The first chapter deals with the poignantly beautiful but sad love affair through which Genji is engendered. Murasaki here borrows from Chinese literature and a poem by Po Chü-i about an even sadder love affair involving a Chinese emperor and a favorite concubine. The birth and early years of the young prince are set against the background of his mother's early death and the deep grief of his father and his mother's mother. The next chapter deals with a small gathering of young nobles sitting together on a rainy night and discussing the qualities most desirable in a woman.

The rest of the work draws heavily on these two chapters. The combination of passion and sadness surrounding Genji's early years frames the love pursuits of his ardent youth and maturity as he searches for the woman who can best satisfy the desiderata set forth by his friends on that rainy night.

The great love of Genji's early years, Fujitsubo—who replaces his mother as his father's favorite—possesses elements of his mother and close ties with his childhood. She bears him a child all think his father's. The great love of his life, Murasaki, is his ideal mate, possessing the various womanly arts and virtues he prizes largely because he himself brought her up as his ward

when she was too young to marry. Set against these two benevo-
lent influences are the Lady Rokujō, whose love for Genji is
combined with a jealousy so virulent it kills, and Lady Kokiden,
a sort of wicked stepmother who is his father's most powerful
concubine and mother of his elder brother, the crown prince.

There are the lesser women, all capable of causing Genji more
or less pleasure, more or less turmoil. The Lady Yūgao dies,
possessed by the avenging spirit of Rokujō. The Princess Asagao
keeps Genji at arm's length all their lives. There is also the
Lady of Akashi, whose father's incantations to the God of
Sumiyoshi bring her and Genji together to conceive a child
who will later become empress.

Ladies of even lesser moment include the Lady Oborozukiyo,
who contributes to Genji's exile; the Lady Suyetsumuhana,
whose red nose goes well with her lachrymose character and
execrable taste; the Lady of the Falling Flowers, whom Genji
once loved but later only converses with; the Lady Tamakatsura,
daughter of Yūgao, who spurns Genji's advances and makes
him feel his years. And finally there is the Lady Nyosan, Genji's
niece, born to a concubine of his brother while the brother
was emperor.

Genji marries Nyosan in his late years at his brother's request,
thus giving her a rank higher than Murasaki, whom he still
loves too much to neglect. As a result, it is Nyosan who is
neglected and, seduced by a young nobleman, bears a child
Genji knows is not his. The novel does not touch on Genji's
possible realization then as to what his father might have
thought about Fujitsubo's child earlier. Japanese fiction is rich
with possible internal recriminations that are not brought to
the surface.

The last third of the novel is concerned with the adventures
of Genji's grandson Niou—son of the empress born to the Lady
of Akashi—and Genji's so-called son Kaoru—Nyosan's child
—and three daughters of Prince Hachi no Miya, an uncle of
Genji, at Uji. Niou, like Genji, is artistic, affectionate, and sexually amoral. Kaoru is serious, religious, and sexually scrupulous.

The result is predictable, although Lady Murasaki's art is
never completely so. Niou takes one of the girls for a wife and
shares another with Kaoru until she succumbs to a fox-

possession and ends up in a nunnery. The third and oldest girl, Agemaki, is sought by Kaoru but dies steadfastly turning aside his tenders of love. The book ends in the monastery to which Ukifune—who trusts Kaoru but is unable to get the importunate Niou out of her mind—has fled.

From the monastery the world of the court seems more remote than at any time in the book. The lesser courtiers who come there seem somehow more real than the men of rank the novel has dealt with almost exclusively. The religious life, in pursuit of the Buddha's way, has not yet provided a substitute, but somehow, through the distraught concerns of the twice-burned, four-times-shy Ukifune, an older Lady Murasaki manages to convey the idea that the finite confusions, the daily difficulties of the monastic life are preferable to the infinitude of artistic, physical, and psychological clashes of the court, its denizens, and its environs.

Arthur Waley's translation, completed before much modern scholarship on the Japanese novel was available, is in many ways the foundation on which modern translation of Japanese into European languages is based. It is also a model of early twentieth-century British prose.

6. Sei Shōnagon. *The Pillow Book of Sei Shōnagon* [Makura no Sōshi]. Tr. by Ivan Morris. 2 vols. New York: Columbia University Press, 1967. Vol. 1, 268 pp. Vol. 2 (Notes and Appendixes), 326 pp.

Sei Shōnagon, a contemporary of the author of *The Tale of Genji* (no. 5), served the Empress Sadako in the last part of the tenth century. Her own words, written about A.D. 994 and included in the book, tell best the nature of the strange volume she has written.

One day Lord Korechika, the Minister of the Centre, brought the Empress a bundle of notebooks. "What shall we do with them?" Her Majesty asked me. "The Emperor has already made arrangements for copying the 'Records of the Historian'."

"Let me make them into a pillow," I said.

"Very well," said Her Majesty, "You may have them."

I now had a vast quantity of paper at my disposal, and I set about filling the notebooks with odd facts, stories from the past, and all sorts of other things, often including the most trivial material. On the whole I concentrated on things and people that I found charming and splendid; my notes are also full of poems and observations on trees and plants, birds and insects.

The result is a collection of anecdotes and witty comments (numbering 326 in the Morris translation) that is one of the finest models of Japanese prose. Items are scattered about with little or no order and carry titles like: "Herbs and Shrubs," "Anthologies," "One of Her Majesty's Wet-Nurses," "Things Not Worth Doing," and "Things That Seem Better at Night Than in the Daytime." Shōnagon's wit has an edge to it, and some of her sallies are models of terse wisdom. Her "List of Things That Should Be Short," for instance, includes "A piece of thread when one wants to sew something in a hurry, a lamp stand. The hair of the lower classes should be neat and short. The speech of a young girl."

The book is not only a source of entertainment, but also a compendium of lore of the Japanese court and nation of Shōnagon's time. The full notes and appendixes in the second volume help make the political, historical, and literary references in the translation intelligible to all readers of English.

Arthur Waley has translated some portions of *The Pillow Book* (London: George Allen and Unwin, 1928) into his incomparable prose. However, the Morris edition, also well translated, is more complete and more scrupulously faithful to the available texts.

7. Sarashina, Lady. *As I Crossed a Bridge of Dreams* [Sarashina Nikki]. Tr. by Ivan Morris. New York: Dial Press, 1971. 159 pp.

The title of this translation can be misleading, since the phrase "Bridge of Dreams" is best known as the title of the last chapter of *The Tale of Genji*. The phrase "I crossed a bridge of dreams," furthermore, is important in Tanizaki's well-known story "The Bridge of Dreams." The translator, Ivan Morris, undoubtedly chose this title because the diary, referred to by the Japanese as *Sarashina Nikki*, is noted for its dreamlike quality.

It is the diary of a lady of the court who is neither a literary genius like Lady Murasaki, a brilliant wit like Sei Shōnagon, nor a disappointed wife like the Mother of Michitsuna. The Lady Sarashina, as Morris calls her, is known to the Japanese simply as Takasue's Daughter. Her diary begins with her twelfth year and proceeds to perhaps her last years when, about fifty and widowed, she lives sadly in an old house, thinking of the Amida Buddha and regretting the many years she has spent less devoutly occupied.

The diary is concerned primarily with the lady's associations with members of her household—her nurse, her sister, her father—with a great number of trips to temples, and with a period of residence at the court. It includes many *tanka*, translated in this edition primarily for their prose content. The first paragraph of Chapter Two sums up the tone of the book:

I lived forever in a dream world. Though I made occasional pilgrimages to temples, I could never bring myself to pray sincerely for what most people want. I know there are many who read the sutras and practise religious devotions from the age of about seventeen; but I had no interest in such things. The height of my aspirations was that a man of noble birth, perfect in both looks and manners, someone like Shining Genji in the Tale, would visit me just once a year in the mountain village where he would have hidden me like Lady Ukifune. There I should live my lonely existence, gazing at the blossoms and the Autumn leaves and the moon and the snow, and wait for an occasional splendid letter from him. This was all I wanted; and in time I came to believe that it would actually happen.

The translation is meticulously done in Ivan Morris's best style, with a useful introduction marked by interesting comments on the texts of the work. There are over thirty pages of notes.

8. *Hōgen Monogatari. Tale of the Disorder in Hōgen.* Tr., with an essay, by William R. Wilson. Tokyo: Sophia University Press, 1971. xii, 176 pp.

To read the war tales, or *gunki monogatari*, in chronological order, one should start with the *Hōgen Monogatari*, which is concerned with the earliest of the disturbances that brought the graceful Heian era to an end. The tale is named for the era it deals with, Hōgen (1156–59), and depicts the series of unfortunate events brought about by the machinations of the retired emperor who had ruled as the Emperor Toba from 1107 to 1123. Installing his eldest son (Sutoku) to succeed himself, he then, after eighteen years, manages to force him to abdicate in favor of another son, aged three, who rules for fourteen years. When he dies in 1155, Toba installs his fourth son (Go-Shirakawa) over the objections of Sutoku, who feels it is time for his own son to ascend the throne.

The struggle between father and son breaks into open warfare, with soldiers being brought in from the provinces by both royal adversaries. These soldiers, drawn from the Minamoto and Taira families, had long been competing for the privileges of providing protection for the fastidious court, dominated by a third great family, the Fujiwaras. In the Hōgen War, Sutoku drew his support primarily from the Minamotos, and Toba from the Tairas. The winner of the war—the last part of which is also dealt with in the *Heiji Monogatari* (in no. **26**)—was nominally the court of the ruling emperor, whose palace had been attacked. The real winner, however, was Taira Kiyomori, who emerged as Prime Minister and the obvious power behind the throne. Kiyomori ruled thus until his death, described in *Tales of the Heike* (no. **9**), after which the tide of power shifted to the Minamotos.

The Wilson translation pays meticulous attention to the provenance of the texts employed and the rendering of many difficult phrases. It is heavily annotated. The essay following the translation places the tale in the full tradition of the *gunki monogatari* and its related documents, and examines in detail the various manuscript texts. This essay is followed by seven appendices (translations of documents that illuminate certain events connected to the tale) and by a four-page bibliography of related books and articles in French, English, Japanese, and Chinese. Titles include *kanji* where applicable.

9. *The Heike Monogatari.* Tr. by A. L. Sadler. *Transactions of the Asiatic Society of Japan* 46 (1918), Part 2, pp. i–xiv, 1–278;

49 (1921), Part 1, pp. i–ii, 1–354, with Appendices to Sanskrit and Chinese references and maps (pp. i–xi).

Tales of the Heike is the greatest of the *gunki monogatari*, or "war tales," and possibly the most musical. Its authorship and date of composition are uncertain; and there are many texts, varying as to extent and content. Mr. Sadler gives weight to the conclusions of the Japanese Society for the Investigation of the National Literature that *Tales of the Heike* was composed sometime before the year 1219, in three volumes, enlarged to six, and then twelve by different hands between 1219 and 1252. He also gives support to the statement in *Essays in Idleness* (no. 13) that it was written for recitation with *biwa* accompaniment by the lay priest Yukinaga, who taught a blind priest named Jōbutsu to recite it, during the time of the retired emperor Go-Toba. The *biwa* priests picked it up, working consciously to imitate the voice of Jōbutsu. (The name Jōbutsu seems to be a corruption of Shōbutsu, the religious name of Minamoto Suketoku.)

The translation begins with one of the most famous prose passages in Japanese literature:

The sound of the bell of Gionshōja echoes the impermanence of all things. The hue of the flowers of the teak-tree declares that they who flourish must be brought low. Yea, the proud ones are but for a moment, like an evening dream in springtime. The mighty are destroyed at the last, they are but as the dust before the wind.

(*Gionshōja* is the Japanese equivalent for the Jetavanna monastery in Savatthi, India.) The narrative then resumes with events following the Hōgen war, which brought the Taira family to power greater than that of the Minamotos, whose leader had backed the losing side. The portion of the Sadler translation published in 1918 carries the story through the years of Taira Kiyomori's supreme power over the government until his death at the age of sixty-four. The 1921 passage shows the reviving of Minamoto power, reaching its climax in the battle at Danno-Ura. It then shows the consolidation of that power under Minamoto Yoritomo, and concludes with the death of the former

Empress Kenrei-mon-in, symbolic in a way of the passing of imperial power and privilege in the new feudal age.

The 1921 edition includes a perhaps interpolated section entitled "The Book of Swords," a Shintoist work found in some of the manuscripts, which connects the story of the Gen and the Hei with the events and deities of the *Nihongi* and *Kojiki* through the history of the Imperial Treasures—in particular, the Imperial Sword lost at Dan-no-Ura—and the histories of the swords Hige-kiri ("cuts through to the beard"), belonging to Yoritomo, and Hiza-maru ("cuts through to the knees"), which belonged to his brother, Yoshitsune.

The Heike Monogatari in this voluminous text must be read by any serious student of Japanese literature. There is no Japanese literary source comparable to it—not even *The Tale of Genji* —for richness of historical and fictional themes that recur over and over again in the centuries of Japanese literature following it. There is the story of Kesa and Morito, used later by Akutagawa in his story of that name, the events on which the noh plays *Atsumori*, *Tomoe*, *Fujito*, and many others are based, and countless other happenings, important and minor, presented in the contexts from which they derived their force in Japanese culture.

Throughout, the Sadler translation, which Edwin O. Reischauer accords the rating "reasonably faithful" (no. **26**, p. 385), reads with much more lilt than any of the available renditions of the *gunki monogatari*. Sadler's intent was certainly to bring the work to readers with as much as possible remaining of the emotional force of the *biwa* priests for whom it was written.

10. *The Taiheiki: A Chronicle of Medieval Japan*. Tr. by Helen Craig McCullough. New York: Columbia University Press, 1959. xlix, 401 pp.

The *Taiheiki* is one of the most important examples of the *gunki monogatari*. There are many extant versions of the work, but that used for this translation concentrates on fifteen years of the reign of the emperor Go-Daigo, from 1318 to 1333. It depicts, in a manner that is not completely accurate historically, the three-way political and military struggle among the shogunate (ruled by regents), the imperial house (led by a forceful Go-Daigo), and certain powerful Buddhist orders during the years when the Hōjō regency was losing its supremacy. As the book ends, Ashikaga Takauji, who will become after a time the first Ashikaga shōgun, is making his power felt.

The plot is complex, shifting, and seldom chronological. It is rich, however, with intrigue, combat, and brave words and deeds, and describes harakiri with endless variations. The translation reads well; it is formal in a style reminiscent of some older translations of *The Iliad*.

11. Minamoto Takakuni. *Ages Ago: Thirty Seven Tales from the Konjaku Monogatari*. Tr. by S. W. Jones. Cambridge: Harvard University Press, 1959. xix, 175 pp.

12. *Uji Shūi Monogatari. A Collection of Tales from Uji: A Study and Translation of Uji Shui Monogatari*. Tr. by D. E. Mills. Cambridge: At the University Press, 1970. 459 pp.

The *Konjaku Monogatari* is one of the world's great collections of folk tales. The tales tend to have a religious (Buddhist) tone but cover a wide spectrum between the secular and the devout. Manuscripts show a list of over a thousand tales, divided into three sections: India (171 tales), China (182 tales), and Japan (710 tales).

The Jones volume is a condensation, the tales selected by Serge Eliseef. The language of the translations is sprightly, and a brief introduction tells much about the background of the larger work from which this volume was chosen.

The *Uji Shūi Monogatari*, like the *Konjaku Monogatari*, dates from the twelfth century. The two collections have much in common—stories, and, at times, even phraseology. The Mills volume, however, includes not only a full, heavily annotated translation of the 197 tales of the original, but also an extensive introduction of 130 pages on the *Uji Shūi Monogatari* and the *setsuwa* or folktale tradition, of which it and the *Konjaku Monogatari* are the great centers.

The Mills translation, however, does not have the pleasing

grace of Jones's narrative style, although it is simple and well
adapted to the many purposes of the literature it expresses.
It is in every way a distinguished companion to Sargent's *The
Japanese Family Storehouse* (no. 16), also published by Cambridge
University Press.

13. Yoshida Kenkō. *Essays in Idleness* [Tsurezuregusa]. Tr. by
    Donald Keene. New York: Columbia University Press, 1967.
    231 pp.

Essays in Idleness is a collection of seemingly random observations by Kenkō, a Buddhist monk whom most scholars believe
lived between 1283 and 1350. They are, in traditional fashion,
concerned with the uncertain nature of worldly things and the
evanescence of life's pleasures. But they also evince a sense of
the fitness and propriety of certain forms of behavior, as well
as a fine sense of irony.

The monk's advice ranges over a variety of situations, from
the practical caution not to smell deer antlers ("they have little
insects that crawl into the nose and devour the brain") to the
admonitory ("the intelligent man, when he dies leaves not possessions"). Again and again Kenkō favors the slow and the
cautious: "Avoid contention with others, bend yourself to their
views. . . . " The best way to triumph in backgammon is not
to try to win but rather to play not to lose. Those things are
most pleasurable which are not too clear, like a conversation
barely overheard. Temples should be visited at night enshroud-
ed in darkness when the visitors have left; and marriage is
best when the husband lives apart from his wife and makes
infrequent, unexpected visits. Clarity, familiarity, and arrange-
ment that is too orderly are all to be avoided.

Essays in Idleness is full of charming narratives. One tells of
a man who had nothing, was given a gourd from which to
drink water, and, annoyed by its rattling on the tree when
the wind blew, threw it away. There are also stories of a curious
priest who loved sweet potatoes, of two Zen monks who killed
one another in a fight, and of a poor man who, having had
an iron pot clamped on his head, could not get it off. Each

incident has its own unobtrusive significance or "moral," which is not pressed upon the reader.

Essays in Idleness is a wonderfully charming expression of the Buddhist *via media*—a desultory and sensitive exploring of the often neglected interstices of experience. It has some of the profundity of the religious treatise, with none of the sententiousness, and the reader feels himself in the presence of a most sympathetic sensibility. The translation is graceful and accurate but lacks the vividness of certain less available renderings, one by George Sansom and another by Ryūkichi Kurata in the *Wisdom of the East* series.

14. *The Ten Foot Square Hut and Tales of the Heike*. Tr. by A. L. Sadler. (1928). Paperbound. Rutland, Vermont: Charles E. Tuttle Co., 1972. xii, 271 pp.

This edition is a reprint of the 1928 Sydney, Australia, edition, published by Angus & Robertson. The translation of *Tales of the Heike* is an abridged version of the Sadler edition printed in the *Transactions of the Asiatic Society of Japan* (no. 9).

The Ten Foot Square Hut (Hōjōki) is a Buddhist cross between Thoreau's *Walden* and the Old Testament Ecclesiastes. It is a world-weary man's testimony to the evanescence of worldly pursuits and the efficacy of simplifying one's life and one's habitation to the point where there is room for little save worship, reading, and playing a musical instrument for one's own amusement in environs that command fine scenery, a measure of shrines and temples, and, in the proper season, flowering trees.

The idiom the translator has chosen is that of the King James Bible, in particular Ecclesiastes. The Sadler translation is a delight to read, particularly in combination with Donald Keene's rendition of the same work in his *Anthology of Japanese Literature* (no. 27), in which some passages are translated more precisely, dates are rendered with other Western and Japanese designations, the names of Buddhist deities are rendered in Japanese rather than Sanskrit, and the style is freed from Biblical influence.

15. Ihara Saikaku. *Five Women Who Loved Love* [Kōshoku Gonin Onna]. Tr. by Wm. Theodore De Bary. Background essay by Richard Lane. Paperbound. Rutland, Vermont: Charles E. Tuttle Co., 1956. 263 pp.

16. ———. *The Japanese Family Storehouse* [Nihon Eitaigura]. Tr. by G. W. Sargent. Cambridge: At the University Press, 1959. 1, 281 pp. (Including *The Millionaires' Gospel* [Chōja Kyō] and *The Seventeen Injunctions of Shimai Sōshitsu* [Shimai Sōshitsu no Yuikun Jūshichikajō].)

17. ———. *The Life of an Amorous Woman and Other Writings.* Tr. by Ivan Morris. New York: New Directions, 1963. 403 pp. (Including translations from *Five Women Who Chose Love* [Kōshoku Gonin Onna], *The Life of an Amorous Woman* [Kōshoku Ichidai Onna], *The Eternal Storehouse of Japan* [Nihon Eitaigura], and *Reckonings that Carry Men Through the World* [Seken Munesanyo].)

18. Hibbett, Howard. *The Floating World in Japanese Fiction.* New York: Oxford University Press, 1959. 232 pp. (Including translations from Kiseki Ejima's *Characters of Worldly Young Women* [Seken Musume Katagi] and *Characters of Worldly Young Men* [Seken Musuko Katagi], and Ihara Saikaku's *The Woman Who Spent Her Life in Love* [Kōshoku Ichidai Onna].)

All four of these works, containing translations of Saikaku's writings, provide introductions on Saikaku and his times. They are profusely illustrated. Together they comprise undoubtedly the most concentrated body of translation, commentary, and scholarship available on any Japanese author. The only works by Saikaku translated in their entirety are *Five Women Who Loved Love* (De Bary) and *The Japanese Family Storehouse*, translated with full notes by Sargent. Excerpts from both works are translated and fully annotated by Ivan Morris.

Five Women Who Loved Love, as translated by De Bary, has the flavor of Chaucer or Boccaccio. It deals with five unhappy love affairs and traces the course of these affairs to their usually disastrous conclusions, with frequent and deep analyses of the social and economic circumstances out of which they sprang.

The Japanese Family Storehouse is comprised of many stories of commercial success and failure against the same background.

Both Morris and Hibbett give excerpts from *Kōshoku Ichidai Onna*, a title translated by Morris as *The Life of an Amorous Woman* and by Hibbett as *The Woman Who Spent her Life in Love*. Saikaku here takes up the erotic career of one woman, following it from its youthful heights to hideous old age. Morris alone translates from *Reckonings that Carry Men Through the World*. The two chapters he translates are concerned primarily with year-end activities and some elaborate ruses devised by creditors to avoid the customary New Year's payment of debts.

Hibbett's volume includes some Kiseki translations that point out the effect of erotic profligacies and other aberrations on family fortunes. Sargent also contributes, in his appendices, translations of the important anonymous contemporary background works, *The Millionaires' Gospel* (*Chōja Kyō*) and *The Seventeen Injunctions of Shimai Sōshitsu* (*Shimai Sōshitsu no Yuikun Jūshichikajō*). They delineate clearly the materialistic canons by which men lived during this time of the ascendancy of the mercantile class.

All are brilliant and painstaking translations, and the striking differences the translators come to in rendering the same texts into English cannot fail to impress the reader with the problems of converting Japanese into English, particularly when the Japanese is the poetic style of Saikaku. Each translator has something different to contribute. De Bary's style is perhaps the most graceful; that of Hibbett a close second. Sargent gives the clearest narration of what is happening in the original, and supplies voluminous notes. Morris brings more of the original over into the English text proper.

A quick comparison of parts of Saikaku's *Kōshoku Gonin Onna* by two translators may be instructive in showing the depth of Saikaku's prose and the problems he poses in translation. Morris translates the title of the first book as "The Story of Seijuro in Himeji, The Town of the Lovely Damsel." He then translates the title of the first chapter of that book as "Love is Darkness, But in the Land of Love the Darkest Night is Bright as Noon." De Bary, who published a full translation of *Kōshoku Gonin Onna* seven years earlier in 1956, rendered the title of book one as "The Story of Seijuro in Himeji," and the title of the first chapter as "Darkness is the time for love; love makes night of day." The differences between these passages might make the reader who is unfamiliar with the vagaries of the Japanese language—particularly Saikaku's—doubtful of the ability of one of the translators. Actually, both translations have excellent justification for their disparate renderings, the details of which are too lengthy to present here.

19. Ihara Saikaku. *The Life of an Amorous Man* [Kōshoku Ichidai Otoko]. Tr. by Hamada Kengi. Paperbound. Rutland, Vermont: Charles E. Tuttle Co., 1964. 233 pp.

The Life of an Amorous Man is the masculine version of Saikaku's *The Life of an Amorous Woman* (in nos. **17, 18**). Surely the double standard was never made more evident. Whereas the woman's life runs fairly steadily downhill, the man's life continues to be marked by rises and falls. At the age of seven he first re-enacted imaginatively the fabled yearly meeting of the star Altair with his love, Vega, on the night of the Star Festival. Many years later he is feted by the courtesans of the city as "grand old patron of Kyoto's gay district." Shortly thereafter he embarks, with six other roués, "in search of the Isle of Nyogo, an isolated body of land inhabited solely by women, never to return."

The translation reads well, although the rendering of the Japanese text is free, and at times even bowdlerized. The book is illustrated with attractive prints by Kawata Masakazu.

20. Miner, Earl, tr. *Japanese Poetic Diaries*. Berkeley: University of California Press, 1969. 211 pp. (Including Ki no Tsurayuki, *The Tosa Diary*; Izumi Shikibu, *The Diary of Izumi Shikibu*; Matsuo Bashō, *The Narrow Road through the Provinces*; Masaoka Shiki, *The Verse Record of My Peonies*.)

21. Omori, Annie Shepley, and Doi Kochi, trs. *Diaries of Court Ladies of Old Japan*. With an introduction by Amy Lowell. (1920). New York: AMS Press, 1970. xxxiii, 201 pp. (In-

cluding *The Sarashina Diary*, *The Diary of Murasaki Shikibu*, and *The Diary of Izumi Shikibu*.)

22. Izumi Shikibu. *The Izumi Shikibu Diary* [Izumi Shikibu Nikki]. Tr. by Edwin Cranston. Cambridge: Harvard University Press, 1969. 332 pp.

23. Matsuo Bashō. *The Narrow Road to the Deep North and Other Travel Sketches*. Tr. by Yuasa Nobuyuki. Baltimore: Penguin, 1966. 167 pp. (Including *Oku no Hosomichi*, "The Records of a Weather-Exposed Skeleton" [Nozarashi Kikō], "A Visit to the Kashima Shrine" [Kashima Kikō], "The Records of a Travel-worn Satchel" [Oi no Kobumi], and "A Visit to Sarashina Village" [Sarashina Kikō].)

24. ———. *Back Roads to Far Towns* [Oku no Hosomichi]. Tr. by Cid Corman and Kamaike Susumu. New York: Grossman Publishers, A Mushinsha Limited Book, 1968. 175 pp.

This composite review of editions and anthologies of poetic diaries includes specimens of two somewhat distinct diary forms widely separated in time, in which poetry and prose are combined: the *nikki* of the Heian period, in which the poems are in the *tanka* form, and the poetic diary of more modern vintage, in which the poems are *haiku*. They are given composite treatment here. The diary form is one of the most enduring preoccupations in Japanese literature, hence subtly altered vestiges of the diary survive in much modern Japanese fiction. Earl Miner, editor and translator of one of the anthologies, has combined three of the Heian *nikki* with two of Bashō's poetic diaries. This review itself has been placed chronologically with works of Bashō's time, resulting in anachronism with Edwin Cranston's *The Izumi Shikibu Diary* and Omori-Doi's *Diaries of Court Ladies of Old Japan*, each of which contains works in common with the Miner anthology.

The tradition of the poetic diary began with Ki no Tsurayuki's *The Tosa Diary* of the tenth century, translated here by Earl Miner. *The Verse Record of My Peonies*, translated also by Miner, is a nineteenth-century example of the form. *The Tosa Diary*

is the prose record of a journey, decorated with the *tanka* composed along the way. Bashō's *Oku no Hosomichi*, its title translated variously by Miner, Yuasa, and Corman, is based on
another journey, one undertaken seven centuries later, and it
is interspersed with poems quite different from the *tanka*. These
poems are early examples of the *haiku*, which in the hands
of Bashō were usually formed as *hokku*, or beginning units for
a chain of poems called *haikai*. In *The Verse Record of My Peonies*
(written by the bedridden poet Shiki toward the end of his
losing battle with tuberculosis), the *haiku* has become a unique
and independent poetic form.

The *Diary of Izumi Shikibu* is an early example of the poetic
diary, perhaps the first written by a woman. (Not many believe
The Tosa Diary was so favored in its authorship.) It is certainly
one of Japan's most explicit love stories, its author active sexually
as well as poetically. *The Diary of Murasaki Shikibu* (written
by the author of *The Tale of Genji*, no. **5**), and *The Sarashina
Diary* (see also no. **7**) present a marked contrast with the vivid
sensual involvements of Izumi Shikibu. Murasaki soberly enter-
tains with balanced presentation the court life about her. *The
Sarashina Diary* is the delicate record of a more reticent woman's
approach to court life, to marriage, and to widowhood.

The *Izumi Shikibu Diary*, translated by Edwin Cranston, is
a valuable production, particularly in its scholarly parapher-
nalia—its introduction, its full notes (including *kanji*), and its
bibliography. The prose is graceful although a little heavy—in
fact both Miner and Cranston seem to attempt at times to imitate
the style of Arthur Waley, their own time and native idioms
notwithstanding.

Miner's *Japanese Poetic Diaries* presents clear translations preceded by a fine introduction, which discusses the genre of the
poetic diary. It draws together the tradition of the form throughout Japanese literature, differentiates the poetic diary from forms
similar to it, and establishes the close affinities of the poetic
diary with not only the tale (*monogatari*) of classical Japanese
literature, but also the novel of more recent times. The introduction also treats with great critical sophistication the subtleties
of authorial point-of-view used in the diaries printed with it.

Although the partial translation of *Oku no Hosomichi* by

Donald Keene included in his *Anthology of Japanese Literature* (no. 27) is perhaps the strongest prose and poetic rendering of that document, the Yuasa translation is very effective. Cid Corman's poetic rendering of the same work, however, must not be dismissed because it differs so vastly from the other renditions. As Miner shows well in his introduction, the poetic values of the poetic diaries cannot be neglected; and if Corman makes too much of them, many other translators fall short in their refusal to depart from the safety of the English prose sentence.

The short selections in the Penguin collection are all fine examples of the form. All travel pieces, they show the poet Bashō well in the two elements Earl Miner sees as the principal concerns of the poetic diary: poetry and time.

25. Jippensha Ikku. *Shank's Mare: Japan's Great Comic Novel of Travel and Ribaldry* [Hizakurige]. Tr. by Thomas Satchell. (1929). Paperbound. Rutland, Vermont: Charles E. Tuttle Co., 1960. 415 pp.

Shank's Mare, first published in Kobe in 1929, is a translation of the Tōkaidō section of *Hizakurige* ("a journey on foot"), the classic Japanese comic novel of travel and ribaldry. Written by Jippensha Ikku (1765–1831) between 1802 and 1809, *Hizakurige* is related to the picaresque tradition, a novel of the rogue and the road, but it is much closer in its earthy, coarse, somewhat scandalous tone to the Spanish picaresque than to the later picaresque of *Tom Jones* and *Huckleberry Finn*. Again we have vital, irrepressible rascals of low degree, existing by their wits, entertained by all that they encounter, and managing to encounter all the great variety of Japanese life on the Tōkaidō, the main road, regulated by military checkpoints, connecting Edo (Tokyo) and Kyoto.

The incidents are generally low-keyed and, except for the connecting strand of the road, the narration is episodic. Yaji and Kita, earlier referred to, participate in various pranks, hear and tell stories, enjoy practical jokes, laugh satirically at the people they meet, satisfy their senses in all ways. What happens to them at each state of the Tōkaidō is governed somewhat by the particular character and tourist attractions of the place. In this respect *Hizakurige* can serve, and was written, as a sort of comic but practical guidebook for the journey from Edo to Kyoto. However, Yaji and Kita do not follow the Tōkaidō without deviation. At Yokkaichi, the forty-third stage of the fifty-three on the highway, they leave the main road for a trip to the Grand Shrine at Ise and for a visit to Osaka, thus missing eleven stages of the Tōkaidō. But the trip to Ise and Osaka provides variety without detracting from atmosphere and tone.

The Tuttle edition of *Shank's Mare* is illustrated by the seldom-seen fifth version of Hiroshige's great series of prints, *The Fifty-three Stages of the Tokaido*, particularly appropriate because Hiroshige (1797–1858) was a contemporary of Ikku and depicted in his prints scenes of the same period that Ikku describes in his travelogue. The Tuttle edition is a handsome one, with wide-spaced type and the complete set of Hiroshige prints. Each of the fifty-five prints (the fifty-three stages plus the initial and final prints for Edo and Kyoto) is attached to a page blank, with a brief commentary. The effect is that of a very lovingly made book.

One is somewhat distressed to find occasional typographical carelessness (is it "Shanks' Mare," "Shank's Mare," or "Shanks's Mare"?) and to find that the translation is occasionally inept. One must, however, admire the energy, perseverance, and skill which are evident in most of the translation by Thomas Satchell, who was born in London in 1867 but lived in Japan from 1899 until his death in 1956. The original Japanese is said to be highly colloquial and dialectal, and Satchell's translation appears to effectively convey subtle jokes and satire.

(This review was written by the late Lois Teal Hartley and published in *Literature East & West* 6 (Winter, 1962). The authors use it in memory of her contributions to the cause of Asian literatures in English before her death in 1968.)

26. Reischauer, Edwin O., and Yamagiwa, Joseph K., trs. *Translations from Early Japanese Literature*. Cambridge: Harvard University Press, 1951. 467 pp. (Including *The Izayoi Nikki, The Tsutsumi Chūnagon Monogatari, The Ōkagami,* and *The Heiji Monogatari*.)

Translations from Early Japanese Literature is the first important example of the translation–commentary, which presents the translated Japanese classic with introduction and prolific notes, a form of publication which as used by Japanese scholars for explanation of classical texts in the modern idiom, is historically one of the wonders of Japanese scholarship. The Reischauer–Yamagiwa volume is extremely useful, not least because of its use of printed *kanji* in the text as well as the commentaries. What the London *Times Literary Supplement* would call "rebarbative" square brackets do crowd the translations, making a kind of obstacle course for the flow of the text, but in many ways this work is a distinguished harbinger of the 1960s and 1970s when the translation–commentary is coming into its own in the West.

The Izayoi Nikki, or "The Diary of the Waning Moon," is in the tradition of the poem-tales (*uta-monogatari*, see page 5–6). It was written by the nun Abutsu (1233?–1283), the last important woman poet of ancient Japan, and the wife of Fujiwara Tameie, compiler of the *Shinkokinshū*, perhaps the greatest of the imperial poetry anthologies. The diary is a four-part documentation of a two-week trip taken by the poet from Kyoto to Kamakura. The first part relates in poetry and prose the preparations for the trip, the second describes the trip itself. The third part draws from the correspondence sent home during the trip. The fourth is a long poem, or *chōka*, of about one hundred fifty lines which has been translated line by line. *The Izayoi Nikki* has a valuable introduction by the translator, Reischauer, which is almost as lengthy as the work it precedes. In this introduction the work is placed in the general artistic context of classic Japanese literature, and the poet is placed in the artistic, social, and legal context of her times.

The Tsutsumi Chūnagon Monogatari, or "Tales of the Lesser Commander of the Embankment," is a collection of ten tales by an author whose identity is disputed. Each tale is seven to fifteen pages in length in this heavily annotated translation. The plots, frequently very slight, vary but are primarily related to love relationships in and about the imperial court. The best-known is undoubtedly "The Lady Who Loved Worms." The translation is by Reischauer; the introduction is by Yamagiwa.

The Ōkagami, or "The Great Mirror," written about 1025, is in the tradition of the historical tale (*rekishi monogatari*, see page 10), which enjoyed its vogue from early in the eleventh century until late in the eighteenth century. The historical tale was a kind of *roman à clef*, with much more emphasis placed on historicity than narrative appeal. It was usually written shortly after the last event narrated had transpired. The selection of *The Ōkagami*, translated by Yamagiwa, deals primarily with Fujiwara Michinaga (966–1027), one of the most influential men in Japanese history, during its most influential years. The result is rather like a candid campaign biography, filled with narrations of the ins and outs of Heian politics: genealogy, status, political in–fighting, religion, poetry, romance, parentage of sons, even archery. The organization is somewhat haphazard, written in a style difficult to read. And in this translation it is made more difficult by the unusually heavy use of brackets to interpolate words and phrases necessary in modern English although unexpressed in Heian Japanese.

The Heiji Monogatari, or "The Tale of the Heiji," is one of the great war tales (*gunki monogatari,* see page 6) which became popular in the thirteenth century. It is concerned in this translation with the first part of the wars between the Taira (Hei) and Minamoto (Gen) factions, and concentrates on the events of the winter of 1159–1160, from which the Taira family emerged victorious. The plot of the tale is based on revolt of the forces of one Fujiwara Nobuyori against imperial authority represented by the monk Fujiwara Shinzei. After Shinzei's death, Nobuyori rules for a time, holding the emperor and former emperor in a kind of house arrest. The emperor escapes, dressed as a lady-in-waiting, and Nobuyori is vanquished and killed by Taira clan forces commanded by Taira Kiyomori.

Edwin Reischauer selected only this first third of the work to translate. It includes the text of the first scroll of the tale and proceeds with the text of the second scroll to the end of the Battle of the Taiken Gate. The translated text thus embraces the subject matter of the three great *Heiji Monogatari* scroll paintings (the first of which is in the possession of the Boston Museum). The texts written on all three paintings are translated in an appendix, with the pictorial contents described and cross-referenced. The narrative, in spite of the bracketed interpolations, is a testimony to the clarity of Reischauer's prose. Especially effective in helping the reader follow the story is the subordination of two digressions in the first scroll by a quick summation of their contents in smaller typeface.

For the past twenty years the book has been a model of Japanese literary scholarship. It is very useful not only to scholars of Japanese history and literature but also of inestimable value to readers who come to ancient Japanese literature with the wish only to be edified and informed.

27. Keene, Donald, ed. *Anthology of Japanese Literature*. New York: Grove Press, 1955. 444 pp. (Paperback, Evergreen Books).

This pioneering anthology, sampling Japanese literature from its beginnings to the time of the restoration of imperial power and the opening of Japan to the West in 1868, has become, with Keene's *Modern Japanese Literature* (no. **114**), the standard anthology of the subject. There are 60 pages from the Ancient period (to A.D. 794), 116 pages from the Heian period (794–1185), 52 pages from the Kamakura period (1185–1333), 103 pages from the Muromachi period (1333–1600), and 112 pages from the Tokugawa period (1600–1868). The translations of prose, poetry, and drama are by many scholars, including the editor; and all are models of their genre. There is a general critical introduction and a short bibliography. Each selection is preceded by a short introduction to the work and the author and each work is identified by title in English translation and romanized Japanese. Most poems are presented similarly, in translation and in romanization.

Arthur Waley's translation of *The Tale of Genji* is represented by a thirty-page episode of Prince Genji's ill-fated affair with a lady called Yūgao. Several other works like *The Tale of Genji* are excerpted in the text in poetry and prose, along with a number of the diaries and prose miscellanies that resemble them. They include *The Tales of Ise*, *The Gossamer Diary* (referred to as the *Kagerō Nikki*), *The Tosa Diary*, *The Pillow Book of Sei Shōnagon*, *The Diary of Murasaki Shikibu*, *An Account of My Hut*,

The Sarashina Diary, Essays in Idleness, and *The Exile of Godaigo.* There are also two *haiku*-prose diaries, one by the greatest *haiku* master, Matsuo Bashō, *The Narrow Road to Oku,* and the other by Bashō's disciple Makai Kyorai, who plays Boswell to Bashō's Samuel Johnson in a piece entitled *Conversations with Kyorai.* Both are translated by Donald Keene.

Folklore is represented in selections from *Tales of the Uji Collection* and a passage from the ancient *Kojiki,* or "Records of Ancient Matters." The worldly and sensual prose of Ihara Saikaku is translated in two passages. There is a short excerpt from the ribald picaresque story of the travels of two ne'er-do-wells on the old Tōkaidō road from Tokyo to Kyoto, *Hizakurige,* and a shorter passage from Takizawa Bakin's lengthy early nineteenth-century novel, *The Biographies of Eight Dogs.*

This anthology is an excellent introduction to the study of Japanese literature in its many phases. The selections are too brief, however, for sustained reading, and may confuse the beginning reader. Particularly recommended are the selection "Yūgao," from *The Tale of Genji,* the passage from *Hizakurige,* and the selections by Ihara Saikaku. The reader who wants more depth should consult the selections on and by Bashō, the section on the noh drama, and the five consecutive chapters on Heian ladies, "Kagerō Nikki," "Yūgao," "The Pillow Book of Sei Shōnagon," "The Diary of Murasaki Shikibu," and "The Sarashina Diary."

Meiji Literature and After (1868 to Present)

28. Mori Ōgai. *The Wild Geese* [Gan]. Tr. by Ochiai Kingo and Sanford Goldstein. Rutland, Vermont: Charles E. Tuttle Co., 1959. 119 pp.

Mori Ōgai, a seminal figure in Meiji literature, was one of the first Japanese writers to study abroad and assimilate the mood and technique of European fiction. *The Wild Geese* is a simple, poignant story of a medical student, Okada, and a beautiful girl, Otama, who becomes the mistress of a moneylender. The daughter of a poor old candy seller, Otama feels acutely the disgrace of being kept by a man of dubious profession and is scorned by her neighbors. The moneylender, however, is delighted with his lovely acquisition, scrupulously keeping all knowledge of her from his suspicious wife.

Okada dreams of encountering the kind of woman found in old Chinese romantic tales—a woman living in virtual seclusion who "makes beauty her sole aim in life so that, with perfect ease, she goes through an elaborate toilet even while the angel of death waits outside her door." Otama, lonely and isolated, one day notices Okada passing by her door. They observe one another fleetingly, and she begins to wait each day for his passing. One evening when the moneylender is away, she dresses with special care, hoping Okada will spend the night with her. Instead he goes out with his friends to a park, where they capture a wild goose to bring home and eat. Soon after, Okada leaves for Germany to continue his studies, and the two never see each other again.

The Wild Geese, beautifully translated, is full of realistic details describing student life and the streets of Tokyo while it remains suffused with the evanescent quality of a love that never materializes. It is one of the most compelling love stories in modern Japanese fiction.

29. Mori Ōgai. *Sanshō-Daiyu*. Tr. by Fukuda Tsutomu. Tokyo: Hokuseido Press, 1952. 72 pp.

This novella is set in medieval Japan and retells an old folktale about a mother and her two children who set out to join their father, a provincial governor. On the way they are kidnapped and enslaved. They are treated harshly and the mother is separated from her children. The boy finally escapes but his sister commits suicide. Years later the boy is reunited with his mother.

This simple, moving story has been made into a fine motion picture, *The Bailiff*, by the talented Japanese director Mizoguchi. Unfortunately, this translation gives little evidence that *Sanshō-Daiyu* was written by one of Japan's greatest writers.

30. Futabatei Shimei. *Japan's First Modern Novel: Ukigumo*. Tr., with critical commentary, by Marleigh Grayer Ryan. New York and London: Columbia University Press, 1967. 381 pp.

Futabatei Shimei (1864–1909) is the first modern Japanese novelist and the first strongly influenced by Tsubouchi Shōyō (see p. 15). The result is a work that captures the sense of loneliness that has become one of the pervading characteristics of Japanese fiction. The translation of *Ukigumo* (Drifting Cloud) is prefaced by extensive critical material, including a sketch of the author's life and an account of the literary climate of the time of the novel's publication. Futabatei's association with Tsubouchi, his interest in the Russian novel, and his translations of Turgenev are discussed in relationship to *Ukigumo*.

The main character is a young man, Bunzo, reminiscent of Turgenev's vacillating heroes. After the death of his father and the consequent blighting of his prospects, Bunzo has come to Tokyo to live with his uncle's family and work as a government clerk. His aunt barely tolerates him, and is angered when she discovers that he has lost his position. The family think it possible that Bunzo will marry his cousin, Osei, but the aunt does all she can to discourage his suit. The uncle is rarely at home, so Bunzo finds the atmosphere doubly hostile. He is a sensitive young man, his pride easily wounded, and instead of resigning himself to his aunt's snubs he broods about her treatment of him.

Bunzo's former colleague, Noboru, is more unscrupulous than Bunzo and gains a promotion. Visiting at the house, he is attracted to Osei. Osei's feelings have not been made entirely clear from the beginning, but as the story progresses she grows to resent Bunzo, and her admiration is directed toward his more successful friend. Noboru offers to use his influence to have Bunzo reinstated as a clerk, but since the offer is made in the presence of Osei, Bunzo interprets it as an insult.

The final chapters of the novel are ambiguous. Noboru seems to lose interest in Osei, who then makes vague overtures to Bunzo. Although Bunzo begins to feel he may have misjudged her after all, their relationship and Bunzo's future are left unresolved.

Japanese critics disagree as to whether the novel, as it stands, is really complete. In many ways it reads like the beginning of a novel, not a finished work. Nevertheless, the historical importance of the work is great; it is the first modern Japanese novel, written in colloquial rather than literary language, and the first to create believable everyday characters and situations. It is certainly not as impressive as Futabatei's other novels, *Mediocrity* and *An Adopted Husband*, but the delineation of Bunzo's tortured pride is penetrating and memorable.

31. Futabatei Shimei. *An Adopted Husband* [Sono Omokage]. Tr. by Mitsui Buhachiro and Gregg M. Sinclair. (1919). Westport, Connecticut: Greenwood Press, 1969. 275 pp.

An Adopted Husband is a moving study of a man so bound by obligations that any course of action seems disastrous to him. The title refers to the Japanese custom of adopting a promising young man to carry on the family name when there is no male heir. Tetsuya, the hero of the novel, has been adopted into the Ono family in order to preserve the family name and restore its dwindling fortunes. As a part of the adoption process, he is married to the daughter of the family, a superficial woman he does not love. To make matters worse, his own prospects have faltered. While his less talented contemporaries have advanced to important positions, he finds himself an underpaid university instructor, saddled with an extravagant wife and mother-in-law and forced to work at several jobs to support them in a style they take for granted. The only ray of light in Tetsuya's drab life is his wife's half-sister, Sayo-ko, the illegitimate daughter of his deceased father-in-law. Sayo-ko was forced to work as a governess at the house of a lecherous, wealthy man, but frightened by his advances, she returns to her family, where she is also mistreated.

The novel is suffused with a sense of irresolution and futility. Sayo-ko and Tetsuya love each other and decide to break away and marry, but the greed and possessiveness of the Onos make this impossible. The lovers have a few moments together, but Sayo-ko finally hides herself from Tetsuya who, in despair, goes to China, becomes a drunkard, and finally disappears. His fate is contrasted with that of another member of the family whose single-minded ambition brings him great success.

Futabatei was a translator and admirer of Turgenev, and the hesitant, febrile quality of Turgenev's heroes clearly had a great influence on his writings. The novel is a fine, skillful rendering of character and situation.

32. Futabatei Shimei. *Mediocrity* [Heibon]. Tr. by Glenn W. Shaw. Tokyo: Hokuseido Press, 1927. 195 pp.

This novel is told in the first person by a man who views his life as a continual series of frustrations in which every action incurs a new burden of shame. The narrator Furuya, almost forty, is a man whose life is summed up by the book's title: "Thinking that nothing can be more suitable than 'Mediocrity' for the title of a description of half a lifetime of mediocrity written by a mediocre man with a mediocre brush, I fix upon that as the title."

Having sent his wife and child to stay with relatives, Furuya reviews the course of his life. An incident from his childhood still affects him most deeply, the death of his dog, Pochi, the only creature he has loved wholly and unashamedly. All philosophizing about life seems empty and sterile compared with the memory of his dog, which had been killed brutally.

As a young man in Tokyo studying law, he lived with an aunt and uncle, and is attracted by their daughter, Yukie San. Although the uncle owed a debt of gratitude to his nephew in return for family favors, he treated Furuya badly, demanding an exaggerated degree of respect, and even insisting that he help with the housework. Yukie San toys with her cousin, arousing his youthful passion only to reject his advances.

Furuya, a man of powerful sexual drives, rejects the idea of Platonic love. Abandoning study of law he becomes a writer, has some success, but finds that the writing profession cannot support him. Although attracted to another woman, his love for her is forestalled by feelings of guilt for neglecting his parents. His father has lost his health and position and lives in poverty. When Furuya returns home to find his father dead, he is overwhelmed by doubts. Having lost touch with the realities of life, nothing seems of any permanent worth.

Mediocrity is a more profound study of a superfluous man than *The Drifting Cloud* but less successful as a novel than *The Adopted Husband*. The narrator's feelings are so diffused and amorphous that the work is as tentative as the protagonist's disconnected musings. It is, however, clearly Futabatei's most agonizingly personal work.

33. Ozaki Kōyō. *The Golden Demon* [Konjaku Yasha]. Tr. by A. and M. Lloyd. Tokyo: Seibundo, 1905. 562 pp.

Ozaki Kōyō was a contemporary of Futabatei Shimei, and *The Golden Demon* is a significant early example of modern Japanese fiction. It tells the story of two thwarted lovers. Kwanichi is to become the adopted son of a respected family, and husband of Miya, the daughter of his benefactor. Her father, however, insists that the engagement be broken so Miya may marry a wealthy man.

The separation of the two lovers ruins both their lives. Kwanichi expresses his disgust for mankind by apprenticing himself to a moneylender, a profession despised for its inhumanity. Miya, on the other hand, is unhappy in her marriage and suffers guilt for allowing her father to arrange the union.

Kwanichi's bitterness increases and, when his employer is burned to death, he takes over the business. At the same time, he is wooed by an unscrupulous woman, whom he despises. When Miya discovers what has become of her former lover, she tries to tell him of her sorrow. Kwanichi, unrelenting in his sense of rejection, his misanthropy unabated, is somehow touched by the plight of a young couple about to commit suicide and offers them the money that will save their lives—and with this act the "demon" turns "golden." The novel ends sadly with Miya looking forward to her death, bitterly regretting the choice that has condemned her to despair.

The title page says the novel is "rewritten in English," but the liberty the translators allowed themselves seems to have produced little stylistic grace. The result is an awkward literary performance, strident and unbalanced.

34. Natsume Sōseki. *I Am a Cat* [Wagahai wa Neko de Aru]. Tr. by Shibata Katsue and Kai Motonari, in collaboration with Harold W. Price. Tokyo: Kenkyusha, 1961; London: Peter Owen, 1971. 431 pp.

I Am a Cat is a leisurely, loosely organized book told from the idiosyncratic perspective of a cat who observes humankind with bemused interest. The cat has been taken in by an English teacher named Kushami, a thoroughly eclectic man interested in drawing, archery, and playing the violin. He has a number of friends who often visit him—a learned proponent of Zen, a man interested in the arts, and a scientist of sorts—and much of the book is concerned with the conversations of this heterogeneous and talkative group. Kushami has a wife and three daughters, whom the cat examines with a rather jaundiced and unappreciative eye.

What little plot there is concerns the narrator's love for the pampered cat of a neighbor and the attempt of a nouveau riche family who live nearby to lure one of Kushami's friends into marriage with their daughter. The real interest of the novel lies in the lengthy conversations of the circle of friends about all manner of things. Kushami notices, for instance, that his wife has begun to lose her hair in one spot. This leads to a discussion on baldness, which includes an account of Aeschylus's death, when a bird mistook his bald pate for a stone and dropped a crab on it to break the shell. Kushami knows many stories about figures in Western history, which he retells, not always fully understanding them, to his friends as examples of a different way of life. Ultimately the cat sips some beer left over from a party, falls into a cistern, and drowns, fortuitously ending the novel.

I Am a Cat is a deft, humorous work, perhaps too long to sustain its comic effects through some four hundred pages, but of interest as an example of the first impact of Western ideas, if only half-digested, on admiring Japanese intellectuals.

35. Natsume Sōseki. *Botchan*. Tr. by Alan Turney. Tokyo: Kodansha International; London: Peter Owen, 1973. 63 pp.

This comic novel is Sōseki's first treatment of a willful and frustrated hero. Botchan (whose appellation might be translated as "The Young Master") narrates his own story, but he quickly helps the reader to see that, although he is a person of great integrity, he is unruly and extremely quick tempered. Alienated from his family, his only close association is with Kiyo, an old female servant who made much of him as a child. Upon graduation, Botchan reluctantly takes a job as a teacher in a middle school in a small country town. Botchan's mercurial temperament immediately gets him into difficulties. His pupils mock and insult him, and his impulsiveness keeps him from making friends with his fellow teachers. Wholly isolated, he gradually begins to realize that he has misjudged some of his colleagues, especially when he sees how the principal and the dean mistreat them.

The principal and one of the teachers are attracted to the same woman, and the principal arranges for his rival's transfer, hypocritically insisting that the new position will benefit the man. The predicament of the mistreated teacher evokes Botchan's sympathy, and he resolves to expose the injustice. He and a friend wait night after night, and finally catch the principal

and his lackey in a brothel. Honor satisfied, Botchan trium-
phantly leaves the provincial backwater and goes to Tokyo,
finds a position with a streetcar company, and settles down
with Kiyo.

The novel is a humorous treatment of a theme that recurs
in Sōseki's work, the tenuousness and even the impossibility
of meaningful human relationships. Here the mode is comedy,
although the singleminded determination of the main character
and his inflexibility foreshadow the difficulties of the protagonists of later Sōseki novels—*Kokoro*, for instance. The Western
reader is likely to find that this novel reminds him of *Huckleberry
Finn*, or perhaps *The Hoosier Schoolmaster*. Like Sōseki's *Kokoro*
it clearly implies that the upright man, copiously endowed with
emotion, will find it extremely difficult to accommodate himself
to an unjust society. Alan Turney's translation offers a pleasant
contrast to earlier translations of the same work.

36. Natsume Sōseki. *The Three-Cornered World* [Kusa Makura].
Tr. by Alan Turney. London: Peter Owen, 1965; Chicago:
Henry Regnery Co., 1967. 184 pp.

A literal rendering of the title of this novel would be "The
Grass Pillow," which is, as the translator points out, "the standard phrase in Japanese poetry to signify a journey." The work
is a strange mixture of novel, travel book, and personal reflection, much as if Bashō's *The Narrow Road to the Deep North*
had been combined with Kawabata's *Snow Country*. It is a serious treatment of the same isolation suffered by Botchan in
Sōseki's earlier work.

A man just past his twenties leaves the city in order to cleanse
his soul of the impurities of society and create a pure work
of art. His thoughts are of Western writers—Oscar Wilde, Doris
Lessing, Wordsworth, Ibsen—whose ideas, imperfectly assimilated, he applies to his own life. When he arrives at his retreat
in the country, he is struck by O-Nami, the hostess of the hotel
where he stays. An attractive divorcee, she is a mystery even
to those who know her best, a mixture of conflicting qualities.
"She was a person in whom understanding and bewilderment

were living together under the same roof and quarreling. . . . Hers was the face of one who is oppressed by misfortune, but is struggling to overcome it."

From the villagers the artist hears different opinions of O-Nami. In a comic encounter with a barber, the artist hears an account he does not trust. A young priest, still another source of information, has apparently been in love with her. The artist is attracted to O-Nami, but since he is intent on breaking all human ties, he will not let himself fall in love with her, seeing her instead as a marvelously accomplished actress in the Noh drama of life. Finally he observes her meeting then separating from her ex-husband, Kyuichi. He is fascinated by her expression, abstracted but compassionate, as Kyuichi's train pulls away. In a moment of exultation he decides that this is the expression he must paint.

The novel is modest in its aims and subtle in its effects. None of the characters, not even the artist who examines himself at such great length, is ever wholly clear. However, two themes are beautifully rendered: the mystery of others and the need to discard human ties for a genuine inner security. The translator prepares the reader for these themes with an epigraph from Sōseki's own work:

An artist is a person who lives in the triangle which remains after the angle which we may call common sense has been removed from this four-cornered world.

37. Natsume Sōseki. *Mon*. Tr. by Francis Mathy. London: Peter Owen, 1972. 217 pp.

Mon (The Gate) was first published in 1910 and deals with Sōseki's favorite theme, the difficulty of human relationships. The hero is named Sosuke, and his inheritance has mysteriously evaporated in the hands of relatives responsible for it. His marriage—a love match, which carries with it a burden of guilt—is unsatisfactory. Oyone, his wife, was originally promised to Sosuke's good friend, Sakai, and the broken friendship that followed the new love has left Sosuke with unstilled pangs of conscience. Sosuke is a civil servant, and both his working and domestic life have settled into a meaningless routine. Although the love of Sosuke and Oyone has not entirely diminished, their life lacks excitement, and they feel that their betrayal of Sakai is evidenced in their inability to have children. Occasionally, the boredom of their existence is relieved by the threat of unemployment or the friendship of their landlord, but life for the most part continues its humdrum course.

Finally, in an attempt to break this pattern of guilt and sterility, Sosuke goes to a Zen temple, hoping to find himself. He discovers the task too arduous, demanding a deeper commitment than he can give, and he leaves for home, caught once more in the web that formerly encircled him.

Mon is written in the plain, unadorned style which characterizes Sōseki when his work is rendered in English. The detail is precise, and although the novel is not long, it presents a penetrating portrait of modern man ensnared by circumstance. It is best to consider this work along with *Kokoro, The Wayfarer,* and *Light and Darkness* as another chapter in Sōseki's continuing saga of personal laceration and isolation.

38. Natsume Sōseki. *The Wayfarer* [Kōjin]. Tr., with an introduction, by Beongcheon Yu. Detroit: Wayne State University Press, 1967. 325 pp. (Paperback, Charles E. Tuttle Co.).

Kōjin is one of Sōseki's most mature novels. It tells a rather complicated story of a number of loosely related people, most of them members of the same family. Jirō, the narrator, first describes a couple, Okada and Okane, who have a relatively happy marriage in spite of certain incompatibilities. Then Jirō tells of a visit to a friend, Misawa, who is hospitalized with a stomach ailment, and of Misawa's fascination with a girl, now dead, but who continues to haunt his imagination. The girl, separated from her husband, was mentally deranged and had lived in the same house as Misawa. Each evening as he would go out she would follow him to the door, mistaking him for her errant husband.

The narrator's brother, Ichirō, is introduced in the second

portion of the novel. Ichirō's marriage is an arranged one, and his wife, Onao, is strangely uncommunicative. Ichirō interprets her reserve as an indication of infidelity, and this supposition so tortures him that he asks Jirō to test her virtue. Jirō refuses, but a chance storm forces him to share a hotel room with Onao. Nothing happens, but Ichirō is so obsessed by suspicion that his sanity is threatened. In desperation the family persuades Ichirō's best friend to go with him on a journey in the hope of easing his mind.

The final portion of the novel consists of a letter from the friend describing Ichirō's strange state. He writes that Ichirō's mind is a frenzy of uncertainties and contradictions. He is lonely, yet incapable of making contact with anyone. He can believe in no absolutes, yet desperately needs them. Religion attracts him, yet he finds no real belief. The future of such a tortured man must remain uncertain.

The novel, apparently a random collection of incidents and character sketches, is in fact a moving description of Meiji society, plagued as it was by an insubstantiality of values. Although not as accomplished or well focused as *Kokoro*, *The Wayfarer* is a skillful work.

39. Natsume Sōseki. *Kokoro*. Tr. by Edwin McClellan. Chicago: Henry Regnery Co., 1957. 248 pp. (Paperback, Gateway Editions).

Although much of *Kokoro* (which can be translated as "the heart of things" or "feeling") deals with the experience of the narrator, the central character is his friend Sensei (which means simply "teacher"), who through much of the novel is a withdrawn and mysterious figure. The novel is a story within a story. The young narrator is fascinated by Sensei and longs for a more intimate friendship with this courteous but remote older man. At the same time, the young man has family worries, and much of the novel describes his father's illness and death. During this time of grave concern for his father, the student receives a long letter from Sensei, explaining the reasons for his withdrawal from the world. Almost half of the novel consists of this missive.

It recounts how Sensei was cheated out of his rightful inheritance by his uncle and, disillusioned with humanity, began to draw within himself. Later, as a student, Sensei gradually becomes attracted to his landlady's daughter, referred to simply as Ojōsan. At this time a new figure enters his life, an even more self-contained young man he calls K. K is a man with a will of iron who seems the embodiment of defiant resignation. When the two disagree, Sensei's arguments are scorned by K: "I remember that I used constantly the word 'human' in defending my position and in attacking his. K insisted that I was trying to hide all my weaknesses behind this word."

Nevertheless both young men seem on the brink of a lasting friendship when K ceases to respond to Sensei's friendship. Sensei begins to suspect that his companion has also fallen in love with Ojōsan. Quite suddenly K commits suicide in his room, thus revealing to Sensei the depth of feeling in his friend. He proceeds with plans to marry Ojōsan, but discovers that K's death has destroyed the last vestiges of his faith in human relationships. His confession ends with his own plans to commit suicide.

Kokoro, well translated, is a very subtle and extremely moving work. What at first seems a rather awkward technical device of a story within a story gives the narrative an added dimension of meaning. This is a profound story of loneliness with a powerful allusiveness which deserves comparison with some of the finest twentieth-century novels.

40. Natsume Sōseki. *Within My Glass Doors* [Gurasu To no Naka]. Tr. by Matsuhara Iwao and E. T. Inglehart. Tokyo: Shin-Sei Do, 1928. 186 pp.

In this work Sōseki presents a series of random and desultory essays on a variety of topics; visitors and correspondents who make various difficult demands, the death of the family dog, his sick cat, memories of his childhood. The tone is detached and ironic, and the author assumes the posture of a man sitting quietly within his study musing on the events of the world outside.

A photographer insists that Sōseki pose for a picture for his magazine, then alters the photograph to show Sōseki smiling; a woman comes for advice about personal problems; an insistent correspondent demands that Sōseki send him a poem; someone who had attended his lecture complains that Sōseki did not make his meaning clear. All the visitors have in common a desire to lay bare the inner self which Sōseki so carefully keeps hidden.

Memories of childhood dominate the second half of the book. Sōseki recalls that his parents were already well advanced in years when he was born and, apprehensive at the thought of raising another child, had given him to others to raise. When circumstances brought him back home, he thought that his parents were in reality his grandparents. His fondest memory of his mother is of her comforting him after a bad dream. In the final sketch Sōseki opens his glass doors and takes a nap in the spring air.

These sketches might be called impersonal-personal essays. Although they often deal with the most intimate matters, their attitude is one of detachment and unconcern—a strategy devised, perhaps, to conceal intense emotion. The work throws light on some of the themes of Sōseki's fiction referred to before, such as the impossibility of genuine communication and the consequent loneliness of his heroes.

41. Natsume Sōseki. *Grass on the Wayside* [Michikusa]. Tr., with an introduction, by Edwin McClellan. Chicago and London: University of Chicago Press, 1969. 169 pp.

Grass on the Wayside is, like *Kokoro*, a novel of Sōseki's maturity. Written for serial publication in 1915, it has little of the humor found in *I Am a Cat* or *Botchan*, and is generally considered to be his most autobiographical work of fiction. The protagonist, Kenzō, is a writer and university teacher who is vaguely dissatisfied with his life. His internal conflicts are disturbing but not clearly defined, for the novel focuses mainly on the various demands made upon Kenzō by people who insist they have a claim on him.

Kenzō's parents, unwilling to be burdened by another child, had given him up to foster parents, although continuing to furnish financial support for him. Any relationship with his foster parents has been long severed and is almost forgotten by Kenzō when his foster father, Shimada, re-enters his life, now a poor man who demands financial support. Kenzō has limited resources but does offer some help to the insistent old man. This revived association, however, conjures up painful memories of an unhappy childhood and the hypocrisy of the old couple; he remembers his childhood as devoid of love and the constant demands for gratitude made by the couple. Inescapable too is Kenzō's present unhappiness, for he and his wife are badly matched and continue to misunderstand each other. Furthermore, Kenzō's father-in-law, who has never cared for him, also demands money. To complicate matters, Kenzō's brother has had little success in life and is a constant worry.

Although outwardly lacking in warmth, Kenzō does his best to cope with the multitude of claims made upon him. He feels himself to be a failure; yet his very modest success makes him a target for all of these importunate people. Disgusted, finally, by the shameless demands of Shimada, he refuses to see him again but is blackmailed. Kenzō's wife, who cannot understand why he lets himself be used by so many people, is relieved when Kenzō makes a final settlement with the old man. Kenzō, however, replies: "Hardly anything in this life is settled."

Although very little outwardly happens in the novel, it demonstrates again Sōseki's persistent theme that people can never understand one another. *Grass on the Wayside* is brief, low-keyed, and unassuming, but masterful in its portrayal of the harried, uncertain Kenzō who, surrounded by a host of people, is as alone as a hermit in the wilderness.

42. Natsume Sōseki. *Light and Darkness* [Meian]. Tr., with an afterword, by V. H. Viglielmo. Honolulu: University of Hawaii Press, 1971. 397 pp.

This is Sōseki's last novel, left unfinished at his death. Like many of his other works, it deals with the mysteries and dif-

ficulties of married life, of people who live in the closest physical
intimacy without being able to understand one another. It relates
ten days in the life of a couple who have been married only
six months and who are uncertain about their relationship.
Tsuda is a man obsessed with himself, prideful yet shy. His
young wife, O-nobu, wants to love him unreservedly and ex-
pects reciprocal passion. The novel opens with Tsuda under-
going a medical examination. He has a case of hemorrhoids
—which he is assured are not tubercular—that requires an operation. The physical ailment is clearly related to an illness of
the self that also needs attention.

There is a characteristic dearth of action in the novel, for
the focus is upon the interrelationships of the characters.
Motivated by a mixture of genuine concern and a desire to
meddle, Tsuda's sister and the wife of his employer both offer
their advice to O-nobu, while a cynical, self-abasing friend tries
to humiliate Tsuda by telling his wife of Kiyoko, her husband's
first love. The novel breaks off shortly after Tsuda goes off to
a resort to recuperate and unexpectedly meets Kiyoko.

Even in its unfinished state, this is Sōseki's longest novel.
But the lack of a conclusion forestalls any definitive judgement
as to its merits. Critics have compared *Light and Darkness* to
the work of Dostoevsky—whom Sōseki had been reading. But
the "scrupulous meanness" of the dialogue and the slow-moving
tempo of the narrative could only have been redeemed by a
conclusion that would have raised the whole work to a more
powerful level and given some significance to the preceding
chapters.

43. Tokutomi Kenjirō. *Footprints in the Snow* [Omoide no Ki].
Tr. by Kenneth Strong. New York: Pegasus, 1970. 371 pp.

This volume is actually a lengthy account of the author's life.
An important literary figure of the Meiji era, Tokutomi led a
tempestuous existence, was a convert to Christianity, thought
of himself as a disciple of Tolstoy, and in his work reflected
many of the conflicts between the traditional and the new in
the emergence of twentieth-century Japan.

Footprints in the Snow has many qualities of the Western autobiographical novel, and reads like a blend of *David Copperfield* and *Of Human Bondage*. It is a novel of hope, energy, and self-reliance—the story of Shintarō Kikuchi, born in an obscure village, who overcomes serious obstacles and forges a successful career as an author. Shintarō's father, badly treated by his brother, becomes bankrupt and dies, leaving Shintarō and his mother with scant means of support, sneered upon by their fellow villagers. They go to live with Shintarō's uncle, Noda, and his family, and Shintarō receives his first formal education. Noda is the most impressive character in the book, a man of kind heart with a ferocious temper that is always getting him into difficulties.

When Noda proposes that Shintarō marry his daughter and take his name as an adopted son, Shintarō refuses, feeling very deeply the obligation of carrying on his own family name. Having thus angered his uncle, Shintarō runs away, is robbed by pickpockets, suffers the pangs of hunger, and is finally rescued by a miserly moneylender who, in spite of a bad reputation, treats the young boy well. The inhabitants of the village are surprised to find that Shintarō knows the rudiments of English, and his thirst for further education leads him to a Christian college in Kyoto. Although attracted by the new religion, he is hesitant and does not convert until after seeing a friend killed by lightning. He continues his studies, although repelled at times by the inflexibility of Western missionaries in their zeal to spread Christianity. He later returns to his mother and Uncle Noda, finding the old man on his deathbed. Back in the city to make his way as a literary figure, he marries the girl he has always loved. The novel ends on a conventionally happy note.

Footprints in the Snow offers significant insight into the restless, optimistic Meiji world and the impact on it of imperfectly assimilated ideas from the West. But the novel lacks genuine depth and dimension and piles incident upon incident until the reader is wearied by the constant change of character and scene. It is as if one were to read *David Copperfield* or *Of Human Bondage* narrated by an author who did not fully understand them in their historical contexts.

44. Kinoshita Naoe. *Pillar of Fire* [Hi no Hashira]. Tr. by Kenneth Strong. London: George Allen and Unwin, 1972. 200 pp.

Pillar of Fire is a rather biased novel, imbued with social purpose. Shinoda, the hero, is a Christian socialist who opposes the Russo-Japanese war, supports the workers in their struggle against a military government, and is finally imprisoned. In this novel, published in 1904, the author attempted to awaken his countrymen to the injustices of a repressive society. Shinoda is loved by Umeko, the daughter of a wealthy man who wants her to marry the brutal Captain Matsushima to advance his own fortunes. She refuses, disfigures her would-be lover, and gives herself to Shinoda just before he is arrested.

The translator compares this work to Charles Kingsley's *Alton Locke* as a novel of social purpose, but *Pillar of Fire* lacks the excitement of that book and other comparable books, and is much cruder in its approach to social problems.

45. Kunikida Doppo. "Five Stories by Kunikida Doppo." Tr. by Jay Rubin. *Monumenta Nipponica* 27 (Autumn, 1972): 273–341.

Very few of Kunikida's eighty short stories have been published in translation. This is unfortunate both artistically and historically, for his writing is highly reminiscent of that of Ambrose Bierce or Sherwood Anderson. He wrote at a crucial time in Japanese literary history, before Japanese naturalism and the I-novel were well established.

The five stories in this volume are a fine primer to the writing of Kunikida. "Old Gen" (Gen Ōji) is one of the more engrossing stories in Keene's *Modern Japanese Literature* (no. **114**); however, the Rubin translation clears up many misunderstandings that the other translation may have created. "Unforgettable People," (Wasureenu Hitobito) is primarily a series of vignettes. "The Bamboo Gate" (Take no Kido), however, is strongly plotted, though quite similar in its denouement to "Old Gen." The fourth story, "An Honest Man," (Shōjikimono) is a cold-hearted man's frank record of his trifling with an idealistic girl. "The Suburbs," (Kōgai) on the surface simply records the swirl of life around a bachelor school principal. But beneath that surface the story conveys hints of the problems and concerns of people around him that make it a kind of miniature saga. It could easily be expanded and made into a film, as was Hayashi Fumiko's "Downtown" (Shitamachi), a work of even slighter scope.

Rubin's introduction to this separately bound section of *Monumenta Nipponica* is a highly useful short critique of Kunikida Doppo's writings and their place in the Japanese literature of his time.

46. Arishima Takeo. *The Agony of Coming into the World* [Umareizuru Nayami]. Tr. by Fujita Seiji. Tokyo: Hokuseido Press, 1955. 103 pp.

In this unusual book, based upon an extraordinary friendship, the narrator meets, almost by chance, Kinjiro Kida, a fisherman who nurtures an impossible dream of becoming an artist. The book is a fictional sketch in which the narrator recalls his meetings with this man—whom he calls Kimoto—and imagines how difficult his goal of self-realization must be.

The narration begins in the first person but soon shifts to the second person as the narrator tries to recreate the difficult life of a man of talent who must fish for a living while existing among insensitive people who cannot understand him. He describes a fishing boat caught in a storm and the overwhelming impression which the forces of nature must have had upon Kimoto: "There extended in all directions, upwards and downwards, the one endless desolation in which you alone kept breathing and which you thought unbearably lonely and dreadful. . . . Like a taper thrown into a deep well with a sinker fastened to it, your mind increased in its brightness and strengthened its sensibility as it went deeper and was at last about to disappear through the surface of the cold water of death."

All the beautiful, implacable forms of nature deeply penetrate the soul of Kimoto, who tries to express them on canvas. "The agony you have to bear alone—though it may be the painful throes of birth—is your own suffering and is what you yourself alone can cure."

It is hard to classify this work, for it is not so much a novel as the passionate and imaginative presentation of the workings of one mind by another. Although the translator sometimes fails to capture the idiom of the English language, the deeply felt insight into the soul of a gifted but not formally educated man is communicated with skill and understanding.

47. Nagai Kafū. *Geisha in Rivalry* [Udekurabe]. Tr. by Kurt Meissner with the collaboration of Ralph Friedrich. Rutland, Vermont: Charles E. Tuttle Co., 1963. 206 pp.

In this novel, Komayo, a young geisha, returns to her profession after her husband, with whom she lived in the country, has died. She attracts the attention of an ambitious young man, Yoshioka, but turns down his offer to become his mistress, which would have been an opportunity to free herself from her obligations. Her beauty and talent attract a Kabuki actor, Segawa, with whom she falls deeply in love, but eventually he tires of her and decides to marry another geisha with an ample dowry.

There are other characters tangentially related to the story. Nanso is a writer who lives an aimless, lonely life in a moldering old house, cherishing his uncompromising traditionalism as he sees the neighborhood around him become more modern. By way of contrast, another writer, Yamai, lives a dissipated and reckless life. Komayo's employer, Gozan, suffers one disappointment after another. His eldest son, a successful actor, has died; the other son leads a dissolute life and disappears; finally his wife has a fatal stroke. Gozan finally turns his business over to Komayo.

Geisha in Rivalry is a leisurely novel, its main narrative line often broken by a variety of poignant situations and characters. It recreates the world of the geisha, suffusing it with a melancholy sadness that, however, gracefully avoids the tragic.

48. Seidensticker, Edward. *Kafū the Scribbler: The Life and Writings of Nagai Kafū, 1879–1959.* Stanford, California: Stanford University Press, 1965. 360 pp. (Paperback).

This volume contains an extensive account of Kafū's life and a critical commentary on his works, in addition to translations of some of his most important fiction. It is the first comprehensive introduction to Kafū's works, and gives some idea of the scope of the author's achievement. There are excerpts from some longer works—such as a chapter from *Rivalry*, previously translated in its entirety as *Geisha in Rivalry* (no. **47**). Other shorter works are presented in complete translation.

The most impressive works included are *The River Sumida* and *A Strange Tale from the East River*, both novellas of mood and reflection. The former is the story of Ragetsu and his concern about the future of his nephew, Chōkichi, who wants to become an actor against his mother's wishes. Since the boy's father is dead, Ragetsu discourages his nephew's new ambition, but as a teacher of poetry himself associated with the theater he complies half-heartedly to Chōkichi's mother's proddings. When Chōkichi is at the point of death, having contracted typhoid and lost the will to live, Ragetsu realizes his mistake and resolves to encourage his nephew to live as an actor. The plot of *The Sumida River* is not as important as its evocation of old Tokyo's disreputable charm before the time of Westernization.

A Strange Tale from the East River evokes a later and more shabby Tokyo. It is the story of a novelist who has a casual liaison with a prostitute while writing a novel about a middle-aged man straying for the first time outside the borders of respectability. Various experiences, such as being searched by a policeman when venturing into a shabby section of Tokyo, furnish material for the writer's book. The device of the novelist writing about writing a novel is handled with skill. At the end, the relationship with the woman dissolves, the book is unfinished, and life itself is revealed as a transitory thing. Once again, atmosphere and mood are more memorable than plot or action.

The shorter works included, "The Peony Garden," "Quiet Rain," "Coming Down with a Cold," and "The Decoration," are tranquil, if sometimes bitter, evocations of the changes —mostly unfortunate—wrought by time. Western readers are likely to find in Kafū much of what they think is quintessentially Japanese: quiet laments for the passing of the seasons, meticulous creation of mood, a resignation to the evanescence of existence. The stories, gracefully translated, make it clear why their author is considered a major figure in modern Japanese literature.

49. Nogami Yaeko. *The Neptune and the Foxes.* Tr. by Matsumoto Ryōzō. Tokyo: Kenkyusha, 1957. 226 pp.

This volume consists of two lengthy stories. *The Neptune* is the name of a trading schooner whose captain is a young man with deep faith in the deity Kompira, the protective god of sailors. The ship is caught in a violent storm, thrown off course, and the captain and his three-man crew fear that the vessel will founder in the high seas and that their provisions will run out before they can be rescued.

Sankichi, the captain's nephew, has full confidence in the captain, but Hachizō and Gorosuke, the only other members of the crew, are skeptical and demand that the food be divided up. Soon, food exhausted, Hachizō and Gorosuke lure Sankichi into a trap and kill him, with cannibalistic intent. The captain, however, discovers the body of his nephew and buries him honorably at sea. Fearful for his own life, he shuts himself up in his cabin but, when another storm makes the cabin the only relatively safe place on the boat, he takes in the two crewmen. When another ship saves them, the captain, still with faith in humanity intact, asserts that Sankichi died a natural death. His faith in Kompira has proved steadfast throughout the ordeal.

The Foxes deals with another humanitarian, Hagioka, who buys a fox farm in the mountains and lives there with his wife, Yoshiko. Although Hagioka's family disapproves of his marriage, the two live happily together in a rugged but idyllic set-

ting. Taking place in the years before, during, and shortly after
World War II, *The Foxes* implicitly praises this couple who have
turned their backs upon the violence and selfishness of
"civilization." Sacrificing their own comforts, they devote themselves to the raising of silver foxes. Hagioka, however, becomes
tubercular and dies. After the war, Kaba, the only relative who
had approved of the couple's marriage, retires from his post
as an admiral in the Japanese navy and assumes Hagioka's idyllic
life.

If these are both stirring accounts of human feeling in the
midst of mindless cruelty and greed, they may seem a bit naive
to the occidental reader. Their note of affirmation is not convincing in a world of devotion to the self. The rendering into English
is usually clear, in spite of some awkward phrasing.

50. Mushakōji Saneatsu. *Love and Death* [Ai to Shi]. Tr. by Wil-
     liam F. Marquardt. New York: Twayne Publishers, 1958.
     101 pp.

Love and Death is a brief, simply conceived novel narrated
in the first person by an ambitious young Japanese novelist,
Muraoka. He makes the acquaintance of an established writer,
Nonomura, who offers generous criticism of the younger man's
work. During his visits to Nonomura's house, Muraoka becomes
more and more attracted to the older man's sister, Natsuko,
and the two decide to marry. First, however, Muraoka must
carry out his plan of visiting Europe. Much of the novel consists
of their letters. As Muraoka is on his way home he receives
a telegram informing him of the death of his fiancée. He suffers
greatly, but achieves resignation. "The conviction that the
departed is too blessed and too god-like to need the help of
the living is for me at least a great consolation."

Love and Death is an unsuccessful attempt, despite an unpretentious and lucid narrative line. The characters are wooden,
the work is without meaningful conflict, and the affirmative
conclusion is unconvincingly abrupt.

51. Mushakōji Saneatsu. *Friendship* [Yūjō]. Tr. by Matsumoto
     Ryōzō. Tokyo: Hokuseido Press, 1958. 162 pp.

This short, intense novel of the conflict between love and friendship is one of the best known works of Mushakōji, an important member of the Shirakaba School (see Introduction, p. 19). It complements well his only other translated novel, *Love and Death*, also a story of thwarted love.

Nojima, the protagonist, is a sensitive young playwright who falls ardently in love with a young woman, Sugiko. He fears that she is attracted to another man but proposes to her through her brother, who replies that she is not yet of an age to bind herself to any man. In his uncertainty Nojima turns to his good friend, Omiya, who comforts and counsels him. Eventually Nojima learns from Omiya, who has left Japan, that Sugiko is in fact very much in love with him. Omiya, in turn, feels guilty about betraying his friend. Nojima is left defiant and lonely.

The story is valuable mostly for simplicity of narration rather than depth of characterization. It is a moving, if sentimental, narrative that has a number of affinities with works in early European Romantic literature, such as Goethe's *The Sorrows of Young Werther.*

52. Tanizaki Junichirō. *Some Prefer Nettles* [Tade Kuu Mushi]. Tr. by Edward G. Seidensticker. New York: Alfred A. Knopf, 1965. 143 pp. (Paperback, Berkley Medallion Books).

This, Tanizaki's first novel generally available in the West, is also his most representative work. Kaname, the protagonist, is unhappily married to Misako, who is attracted to things modern and Western. Kaname, who himself has acquired a veneer of Westernization, visits a Eurasian prostitute who powders her skin to emphasize her Western characteristics. However, the impending breakup of Kaname's marriage brings with it a growing interest in the serenity of the Japanese past. Ironically, the source of much of this interest is his father-in-law. The old man is a devotee of bunraku, the puppet theater, and when Kaname accompanies him to a performance of this dying art, memories of childhood visits with his mother overwhelm him. In the artificiality of the puppetry, an art long ago frozen into static patterns, he sees at once release and escape from emotion.

Kaname and Misako remain friendly, but Misako is clearly attracted to another man. They have a son, but he does not present an insurmountable barrier to their separation. Meanwhile, Misako's father has a lovely Japanese mistress, O-hisa, an enchanting doll-like girl, thirty years younger than her patron. Kaname finds her fascinating, attracted more by what she stands for than by her individual reality as a person. At the novel's end the father-in-law tries to bring Kaname and Misako together at his house, but he takes his daughter out to dinner and leaves Kaname with O-hisa. As Kaname goes to bed, he is startled by O-hisa's resemblance to a puppet in the corner of the room. Kaname has become thoroughly committed to the old Japan.

Some Prefer Nettles, beautifully rendered into English, is a novel of mood more than of plot. Although less impressive than some of Tanizaki's other fiction, it is a sensitive, fine introduction to the major themes of his work.

53. Tanizaki Junichirō. *Seven Japanese Tales*. Tr. by Howard Hibbett. New York: Alfred A. Knopf, 1963. 298 pp. (Paperback, Berkley Medallion Books).

Although these seven tales deal with people caught in the grip of some obsession, what is most impressive about them is their outward calmness. The three most important stories —"A Portrait of Shunkin," "The Bridge of Dreams," and "A Blind Man's Tale"—are narrated in the first person, a technique used not to clarify the plots but to suffuse the stories with ambiguity.

"A Portrait of Shunkin" concerns a blind girl who is a virtuoso on the samisen. A boy named Sasuke admires her from afar, serves her abjectly, and becomes her pupil. Although she is imperious and moody, he responds to her every wish, loving her with humility and unquestioning devotion. The rather impersonal narrator gathers information from various sources and speculates on the meaning of this strange relationship, but the reader is not bound to accept his interpretations. Some unknown person, angered by Shunkin's proud manner, disfigures her slightly with boiling water, whereupon Sasuke blinds himself so he will never have to witness even the slightest desecration of her loveliness. Their relationship deepens in a world now almost entirely closed to others.

"The Bridge of Dreams" is another story with a claustral setting. The narrator, Tadasu, is a boy closely attached to his mother. When she dies, his father remarries a woman very much like his previous wife, and the three live together, heedless of the outside world. The stepmother is very tender toward Tadasu, even offering to let him suck her milkless breasts as his mother had done long after he was weaned. It is a primal oedipal situation. When another child is born, the father, fearing of diminished affection for Tadasu, has the newcomer raised by others. He also chooses for Tadasu a wife of inferior family so that nothing will interfere with their cloistered life. One day, after the death of the father, the stepmother is bitten by a centipede while being massaged by Tadasu's wife and dies. Tadasu, suspecting his wife of having purposely caused her death, obtains a divorce, and the story ends with Tadasu's plan to reclaim his brother and perpetuate the enclosed family life.

"A Blind Man's Tale" is told by a blind masseuse who narrates his role as observer in the fierce anarchic wars of the sixteenth century. His employer is the wife of Nagamasa and the sister of Nagamasa's sworn enemy, Nobunaga. When defeated, Nagamasa commits suicide, refusing to allow his wife to join him. She returns to her brother, who murders her young son out of vengeance against her husband's clan. She is then wooed by two generals, marries one, and is subsequently widowed in another conflict. Through the involved account of wars, the blind man remains wholly devoted to his mistress—one feels somewhat obsessively. When she finally commits suicide, he flees with her daughter but is scorned by the girl, who had wished to die with her mother. Although willing to transfer his unlimited devotion to the daughter, in whom he sees the image of her mother, he is clearly not wanted and must make his own lonely way in the world.

The other stories are shorter. "Terror" sketches a man afraid of riding on trains. "The Tattooer" is an account of a man who takes pleasure in the thought of the pain he will inflict on a beautiful girl by tattooing a spider on her back. "The Thief" concerns a compulsive pilferer; and "Aguri" is about a young man hopelessly in love with a waitress.

Although the material of these stories is sadism, incest, and violence, their effect is strangely serene. The heroes of the three longer stories desire above all to get into close and uninterrupted contact with the beloved and to shut out the world. Tanizaki transmutes the unpleasantness inherent in such a world into a lovely, if temporary, paradise. The first two stories especially are most impressive, ranking with the finest short fiction in any language.

54. Tanizaki Junichirō. *The Makioka Sisters* [Sasameyuki]. Tr. by Edward G. Siedensticker. New York: Alfred A. Knopf, 1957. 530 pp. (Paperback, Universal Library, Grosset & Dunlap).

The Makioka Sisters, generally recognized as Tanizaki's masterpiece, deals with the lives of four sisters in the years preceding Japan's entrance into World War II. Tsuruko, the oldest sister, is married to Tatsuo, an adopted husband, who has become the active head of the family. She, however, plays a relatively minor role. The novel is most concerned with the three younger sisters, who live near Osaka—Sachiko, who is married, and Yukiko and Taeko, both single. Ostensibly the plot is about the family's continually thwarted attempts to find a suitable husband for Yukiko, who must be married before the younger sister Taeko can wed Okubata, an impecunious son of a socially prominent family. Some years earlier, Taeko caused a minor scandal by attempting to elope with Okubata, and this incident still casts a shadow on the reputation of Taeko and the family. She later threatens the family again by a new association, this time with a bartender.

The novel is organized around a series of *miai*, or formal permarital meetings, in which prospective husbands and Yukiko are brought together. When the novel begins, Sachiko, from whose perspective the reader views most of the action, reflects upon the numerous, always unsuccessful, *miai* of the past, and hopes ruefully that Yukiko, who is no longer young, will put aside her diffidence and family pride. Something seems lacking in every candidate or, if one appears at first promising, the family investigation uncovers some insurmountable barrier in his life. Finally after many disappointing attempts, an acceptable suitor is found in a middle-aged man of good family, an architect and interior designer, but penniless.

Although the sisters are close to one another they do not reveal their innermost thoughts. No one, for instance, is ever sure what Yukiko is thinking. And Taeko, who makes dolls and has set up a shop, has a life of her own which her sisters only discover near the novel's end.

In most novels one event leads unavoidably to another and builds toward a climax and resolution, but not in *The Makioka Sisters*. Events flow into one another, and nothing is really resolved at the end. The family's social station and fortunes are neither saved nor destroyed by the happenings in the novel, and Tanizaki carefully eschews any comment, implicit or open, about his characters or the significance of their tangled associations.

The novel is deeply influenced by *The Tale of Genji* (no. 5), which Tanizaki spent many years translating and twice retranslating into the modern idiom, and moves quietly and unobtrusively, avoiding climaxes and moments of revelation. The narration is entirely lacking in any bias. The author's limpid objectivity gives the work a marvelous feeling of life slowly passing. The characters are not concerned, as they would likely be in a Western novel, with a sense of futility and ennui; instead, they fit silently within the social fabric woven around them. Events of the outside world enter seldom and occasion only the most cursory comment from the characters. Even though *The Makioka Sisters* covers only a few years, it is a family chronicle like *Buddenbrooks* and *The Forsyte Saga*. But while they emphasize the external events of their characters' lives—the births, marriages, and deaths—*The Makioka Sisters* concentrates upon a deeper reality, the slow evanescent progression of ordinary life, which becomes hauntingly real in Tanizaki's pellucid narration. The novel can be read simply as a graphic picture of a merchant family in slow disintegration but lovingly preserving a vanished world, or, on a more profound level, as a novel

which conveys the magic of certain still moments rarely captured
in Western literature.

55. Tanizaki Junichirō. *The Key* [Kagi]. Tr. by Howard Hibbett.
New York: Alfred A Knopf, 1960. 183 pp. (Paperback, Berkley Medallion Books).

The Key is composed of two diaries, that of a fifty-five-year-old
man and that of his wife, Ikuko, who is in her forties. Although
they have been married many years, their relationship has never
been wholly frank or satisfactory. The husband, who has always
resented his wife's sexual inhibitions, now feels his own vigor
flagging. One evening, because of some medicine she has taken
to alleviate an illness, she falls into a deep sleep. The husband,
impelled by a strange desire to feast his eyes on Ikuko's naked
body, exposes her under a harsh light and lavishes silent praise
on her loveliness, so unaffected by the passage of time. He
is not quite certain she is completely unaware of his attentions
but, driven by his passion, he indulges himself nightly in
observing his wife's beauty, faithfully recording his infatuation
in his diary. At the same time, Ikuko, although reticent, makes
clear in her diary that she knows of her husband's strange impul-
sions. Both employ elaborate stratagems to keep their diaries
hidden; but each manages to acquire the other's confession.
Circumspect and even cool in their everyday relationship, they
nonetheless communicate with one another in this fashion.

The husband is driven to drugs in order to maintain this
life of sexual frenzy. The wife is disgusted by her husband's
behavior, but at times imagines him to be the young doctor,
Kimura, to whom she is attracted. Although the husband is
warned that his blood pressure is at a dangerously high level,
he persists in his reckless course until he has a fatal stroke.
In her final entry, Ikuko confesses that she had purposely stirred
his passion and jealousy to kill him. She contemplates with
pleasure the fact that her daughter will marry Kimura and the
three of them will live together.

This short novel is told with highly suggestive restraint. The
husband's strange dominance over the wife is reversed, and

the reader, with shock, realizes that she has always been in control. Tanizaki's finest fiction has always featured a drama of almost cosmic importance played out upon a seemingly tiny stage of domestic conflict, and this work is a masterpiece of the genre.

56. Tanizaki Junichirō. *Diary of a Mad Old Man* [Fūten Rōjin no Nikki]. Tr. by Howard Hibbett. New York: Alfred A. Knopf, 1965. 177 pp. (Paperback, Berkley Medallion Books).

If the husband of Tanizaki's *The Key* had survived to old age, he might well have told this story as a sequel to his earlier obsession. This is the day-to-day confession of a man well into his seventies—the affluent patriarch of his family, impotent and in ill health—who experiences an uncontrollable passion for his beautiful daughter-in-law, Satsuko. Satsuko is very much the modern Japanese woman, cosmopolitan and liberated, and no longer in love with her husband. She tolerates occasional attentions from the old man, including a kiss in the shower and a weak caress. Although she feels no attraction for her toothless and wheezing father-in-law, she hides whatever disgust she feels and trades a few harmless attentions for presents, such as a cat's eye diamond ring and the promise of a swimming pool.

Most of the story is told by the old man, who records his growing obsession with a tinge of self-directed irony. He makes a trip to pick out his burial stone, and there conceives the idea of having Satsuko's footprint on his tombstone (as if she were Buddha himself) so that he might feel the weight of her foot throughout eternity. For this purpose, he takes rubbings of her feet with great pleasure. He suffers a stroke, can no longer write in his diary, and the rest of the story is told through the reports of his doctor, nurse, and daughter. The old man survives in weakened condition, sustained by the thought of seeing Satsuko swim in the pool he is having built.

Although this is the slightest of Tanizaki's novels, and the one in which his penchant for describing masochistic behavior is most pronounced, it is one of the most vivid portrayals of

old age in literature, expressing the daily trials of a person
constantly aware of physical limitations and embarrassments.
Told without sentimentality, its total effect is both harrowing
and ironic.

57. Kagawa Toyohiko. *Before the Dawn* [Shisen wo Koete]. Tr.
     by I. Fukumoto and T. Satchell. London: Chatto & Windus,
     1925. 398 pp.

This translation, which was published in this edition in 1925
and had appeared earlier in Japan under the title *Across the
Death Line*, was one of the first modern Japanese novels to be
translated and published in the West, a fact probably attribut-
able to its religious emphasis. It is the story of Eiichi Niimi,
a young man whose well-to-do merchant father has abandoned
his mother and is living with another woman. Eiichi reads
widely in Western philosophical and religious literature and
is attracted to Christianity in the hope of finding a solution
to his inner conflicts. His anger with his father causes him
deep dissatisfaction with his mode of life. After a half-hearted,
unsuccessful attempt to burn down the family home, he leaves
and finds employment as a laborer, the exhausting work helping
him to escape his mental turmoil.

His father dies, and Eiichi returns to work in the debt-ridden
family business. Still discontented, he decides to live a
genuinely Christian life and goes to dwell in the slums, where
he encounters the dregs of humanity—beggars, thieves, violent
men, and people suffering from disabling and disfiguring diseases. Although his concern is often misunderstood, he persists
in preaching to the poor and trying to help them. He is attracted
to two different women, Kohide, a beautiful geisha, and Miss
Higuchi, a warm-hearted woman who shares his instinctive
love for the downtrodden. The novel ends abruptly after Eiichi's
arrest and subsequent release for helping a group of strikers
present their demands to the factory management.

Before the Dawn is clearly an autobiographical work with a
religious purpose, but it is notably free of self-pity or unctuous
piety. It is a stark, unadorned narrative, in which the message

far outweighs artistic considerations. Nonetheless—or because of this—the novel is a powerful statement on the author's commitment to nonviolent Christian socialism.

58. Nagayo Yoshirō. *The Bronze Christ* [Seidō no Kurisuto]. Tr. by Yada Kenzoh and Henry P. Ward. New York: Taplinger Publishing Co., 1959. 159 pp.

The Bronze Christ is a short novel about the persecution of Christians in seventeenth-century Japan, with an introductory note explaining its historical background. Suspected Christians were threatened with torture and death if they did not renounce their faith by stepping on a Christian image. The main character, Yusa, is a young artist in love with a Christian girl, Monika. His feeling for her draws him to the small society of Christians in the community, but he is not really tempted to become a convert.

He recalls the tortures Monika's people endured, such as being hung upside down so that the internal organs exert pressure on the head. "Then from his mouth, nose, and eyes, some blood would trickle but that way the victim would die rapidly of congestion—in as little as seven or eight hours. In order to prolong death they cut small holes in his forehead and temples to let out the blood."

Ultimately he is called upon to cast a statue the Christians will be asked to tread upon. Inspired by Monika, he responds by creating a beautiful bronze Christ. The work is so fine that the authorities are suspicious: "the dedication you [Yusa] showed in that statue is far stronger, far deeper, and much more awesome than any other believers we have seen as yet." As a result, Yusa is sentenced to death, and the author concludes the novel by stating, "Yusa Hagiwara was never a Christian, not even at the last."

Much of the novel's effect comes from the ambiguity of the conclusion, and it is hard to be certain whether its ultimate meaning is religious or aesthetic. However, it is a moving parabolic study of the artist and the depth of his commitment.

59. Akutagawa Ryūnosuke. *Tales Grotesque and Curious*. Tr. by
Glenn W. Shaw. Tokyo: Hokuseido Press, 1930. 144 pp.

This volume contains eleven stories, including three available
in various other editions—"The Nose," "The Spider's Thread,"
and "Rashōmon." The stories are suffused with Akutagawa's
characteristic bittersweet irony concerning the aspirations and
illusions of men.

"Tobacco and the Devil" tells how a man outwits the devil
and saves his soul by discovering the name of a strange plant
—tobacco—that grows in his field. A comment at the end, however, casts doubt on the effectiveness of the devil's defeat. "The
Handkerchief" depicts a professor at first moved by the grief
of the mother of one of his students who has died, but is later
disturbed by the suspicion that her sorrow, expressed by a
theatrical gesture with her handkerchief, is not sincere. "Lice"
is about a group of lice-infested soldiers. One shocks his com-
panions by collecting the lice, claiming that they keep him warm.
Another disagrees and claims that they are good to eat.
Akutagawa suggests that this useless quarrel over such loathsome creatures is characteristic of man's conflicts. Two other
stories, "The Wine Worm" and "The Badger," are short
sketches, which, like "The Dragon" of a later volume, deal with
the confusion between illusion and reality. The final story,
"Mori Sensei," is a moving account of an old English teacher
scorned by his young students. He loses his position through
incompetence and is seen years later by the narrator, eagerly
teaching the waiters in a restaurant, pitiable but utterly committed to his work.

This is a representative collection of Akutagawa's short fiction.
None is comparable to "Hell Screen," "In a Grove," or "Yam
Gruel." Yet, all are worth reading, each offering a small but
penetrating insight into the human condition.

60. Akutagawa Ryūnosuke. *Hell Screen and Other Stories*. Tr.
by W. H. H. Norman. (1948). Westport, Connecticut, Greenwood Press, 1970. 177 pp.

Akutagawa is a master of the short story, and this volume includes some of his most impressive achievements. The title story concerns an accomplished painter, Yoshihide, who is working on a large painting that depicts the suffering of those condemned to hell. He is an aloof and unpleasant man, an artist who must see what he paints before he can re-create it with his brush. He envisions as the center panel of the screen a burning carriage falling through the air with an exquisite court lady inside. The painter's patron lord agrees to accommodate him by allowing him to witness such a scene, but to the painter's horror he discovers the lady inside is his own daughter. Yoshihide finishes the painting and hangs himself.

"Jashumon" is the longest story, but unfortunately it is unfinished, its resolution not clear. It concerns Wakatono Sama, the son of the ruler in "Hell Screen," and the coming of a Christian "Mary Priest," a sinister figure who seems protected from harm by supernatural power. The story breaks off just as he is besting a group of Buddhist monks in a display of his spiritual powers. The other two stories, "The General" and "Mensura Zoilii," are slight works that satirize the Japanese army and the Japanese literary world.

The title story of this volume clearly proves Akutagawa as a master of skillful and cutting irony. The scope and power of his short fiction are comparable to the works of such European masters as Heinrich Von Kleist.

61. Akutagawa Ryūnosuke. *Kappa*. Tr. by Shiojiri Seiichi. (1949). Westport, Connecticut: Greenwood Press, 1970. 136 pp.

The Kappa is a mythical figure in Japanese folklore, similar in some respects to the fairy of Celtic legend but with more animal-like characteristics. The introductory note to the translation discusses its appearance in Japanese folklore. The story itself purports to be the account of a patient in a mental institution who, while vacationing, falls into the hands of a group of Kappas and is taken to their mythical land. Examining Kappa society, Akutagawa satirizes his own civilization. Sex, business,

and politics are targets of his ironic scrutiny. The visitor wonders
why, since machines are replacing workers, there is no unemployment, and he is told that unemployed workers are "eaten
up." "After all, the state is so good as to save them the trouble
of starving to death or of committing suicide. Just a little poison-
ous gas, you see, and they are done for. So they don't suffer
much pain."

The visitor meets a Kappa philosopher, and reads his worldly-
wise aphorisms, tinged with cynicism. He hears that criminals
are punished simply by being charged with their crime, which
is often enough to kill them. The visitor finds his way home,
but discovers that he misses the Kappas, who live a more honest
life than his fellow countrymen.

Kappa is a kind of Japanese *Gulliver's Travels*, cynical yet amus-
ing, but without the bitterness or depth of insight of Swift's
satire.

62. Akutagawa Ryūnosuke. *Rashōmon and Other Stories*. Tr.
    by Kojima Takashi. New York: Liveright, 1952. 119 pp.
    (Paperback, Bantam Books).

This, the earliest collection of Akutagawa's short stories to
be published in the United States, is perhaps his best. "In
a Grove," the story of a murder recounted by the people involved
in it, was the source of Kurosawa Akira's film *Rashōmon*. A
man and his wife on a journey are lured from the road by
a bandit overcome with lust for the woman. The bandit over-
powers the husband, Takejirō, ties him to a tree, then violates
his wife. The stories of the three principals as to what happened
next vary. In the version of Tajōmaru, the brigand, the wife
insists she cannot live if two men know of her shame, so she
begs him to kill her husband. He frees Takejirō, the two fight,
and the husband is killed, during which time the woman has
disappeared. The wife, however, claims that she and her husband had made a suicide pact. Her husband had honored this
pact but she had failed. Next, the dead husband, who communicates through a medium, recounts how his wife, after her
violation, demanded that Tajōmaru kill him, and that he,

shocked by her request, offered to kill her. After she ran off, Tajōmaru loosened his bonds; whereupon he stabbed himself but received a coup de grâce from behind by someone he did not see. The reader is left in doubt concerning the ultimate truth.

Rashōmon is a gate in Kyoto, and the story so titled concerns the servant of a samurai who, in a time of calamities and famine, stands under the gate and wonders whether he should become a thief to save himself from utter destitution. He is horrified at seeing an old woman pulling the hair from a dead body to make wigs. When he angrily stops her, she tells him that the dead woman herself had sold snake flesh for fish to save herself from starvation. Such behavior, she explains, is the law of life. The servant then angrily tears the clothes from the old woman's body and throws her down the stairs, proclaiming, "Then it's right if I rob you. I'd starve if I didn't."

The third story, "Yam Gruel" (set in the Heian period) is about a hapless samurai referred to as Goi, an oafish figure of fun and the victim of others' jokes. This simple man with a protuberant red nose has but one wish—to eat his fill of yam gruel, which one of his superiors promises to grant someday. Goi is overjoyed at even the remote prospect of fulfilling this cherished wish. One day the lord takes Goi to his estate where he has placed before him a "huge vat filled to the brim with a tremendous sea of yam gruel." Goi cannot begin to eat it all, but the experience destroys the only thing left to him in life. All rebuffs and mistreatment were somehow bearable if he could cling to his secret desire to gorge himself with his favorite dish. Now even this is taken from him.

The remaining stories are "The Martyr," "Kesa and Moritō," and "The Dragon." The first is the story of a monk who is expelled from his monastery for fathering a child. He dies saving the child and is then discovered to be a woman. "Kesa and Moritō," taken from an incident in *Heike Monogatari* (no. 9), is about a woman killed unwittingly by her lover. "The Dragon" is concerned with a monk who for a joke erects a sign predicting a dragon ascension, only to be gradually taken in by his own hoax.

This is the finest of the various collections of Akutagawa's work. The stories included are all of a consistently high level of excellence. Dealing with the evanescence and insubstantiality of human character and motive, they explore the dark and uncertain places of the human soul without pretending to solve their mysteries. One man's truth, Akutagawa seems to say, is not sufficient even to himself. One can never really hope to understand another person.

63. Akutagawa Ryūnosuke. *Japanese Short Stories.* Tr. by Kojima Takashi. New York: Liveright, 1962. 157 pp. (Paperback, Avon Books).

There are ten stories in this volume, including "Hell Screen," the only reprint from the W. H. Norman book (no. **60**). A number of the stories—really short sketches—are interpretations of traditional tales from Japanese history and folklore. "Nezumi-Kozō, a Japanese Robin Hood" is the account of a farcical incident from the career of the figure described in the title. "Heichū, the Amorous Genius" has loved many women but has never been able to devote himself completely to one "because he always carries in his heart a vivid image of a Venus of celestial beauty beyond human attainment." "The Story of Yonosuke" recounts how a Japanese Don Juan sought vainly to suppress his uncontrollable love for an unresponsive woman.

A gloomy, naturalistic story with a contemporary setting, "Genkaku-Sanbō" is about the last days of Genkaku, a land speculator, and his family. Genkaku is dying of tuberculosis. His wife is partially paralyzed and bedridden. Their daughter, Osuzu, suffers for her mother because her father's mistress has moved into the house, bringing with her an illegitimate son to be with the old man during his last days. Akutagawa describes the relationships between these unhappy people and graphically depicts Genkaku dying in despair.

In "A Clod of Soil," Osumi, an old peasant woman, has just lost her only son. Her daughter-in-law, Otani, works the farm, and they prosper. Although Otani works diligently and wins the admiration of the whole countryside, Osumi, having looked forward so long to the leisure of old age, is unhappy and feels condemned to eternal household tasks. Unexpectedly Otani dies, and the old woman is finally free to indulge herself on their accumulated income, only to find that she misses her daughter-in-law deeply.

"Otomi's Virginity" is set during a time of civil disturbance. Otomi remains behind when her family is forced to vacate their house. While she is alone, a beggar enters, is attracted to her, and forces her to yield to him by threatening to kill the family cat. Twenty years later, having by this time attained a position of power and importance, Otomi remarkably recognizes the beggar. She searches her mind to discover her motive in having given herself to him so many years ago but can find no answer.

"The Spider's Thread," "The Nose," and "The Tangerines" are very brief sketches. The first deals with an evil man who because of one, almost inadvertent, good deed in his life, is given a chance to escape hell but loses this opportunity through his selfishness. In "The Nose," a Buddhist priest with an embarrassingly long nose works mightily to shorten it, finally succeeds, and finds he has gained nothing. "The Tangerines" depicts an unhappy man whose life is suddenly cheered by watching a companion in a railway carriage throw tangerines out the window to her waiting young brothers.

None of the other stories in this volume compare in quality with the first, "Hell Screen," but Akutagawa's interpretations of traditional figures are handled well, and his talents as an accomplished master of irony are in evidence in "A Clod of Soil" and "Otomi's Virginity." The language of the translation is not as felicitous as it might be.

64. Akutagawa Ryūnosuke. *Exotic Japanese Stories.* Tr. by Kojima Takashi and John McVittie. New York: Liveright, 1964. 431 pp.

The largest and most recent collection of Akutagawa's fiction, *Exotic Japanese Stories*, includes a number of works (*Kappa*, "Heresy," "The Handkerchief," and "The Badger") that are available in other translations. The longest of the new stories in this volume is "Robbers," which deals with a band of outlaw

samurai in medieval Kyoto. The past is in no way used to roman-
ticize events. The band is filthy and treacherous, and its various
members described in loathsome detail. Perhaps the finest story
is "Withered Fields," depicting the death of the great poet
Bashō. Although the thoughts of the disciples clustered around
his deathbed apparently center on the sadness of his demise,
each in truth contemplates its effect upon himself. One thinks
of his own prospective death, another of succeeding Bashō in
acclaim.

"The Dog, Shiro" is a humorous parable about virtue. In
"Gratitude" a man pays his debt to a famous robber by dying
for him. "The Dolls" is a touching, unsentimental story about
a girl who must sell her exquisite dolls to support her family.
There is also a short narrative, "The Lady Roku-no-Miya," about
a deserted lady whose spirit wanders, held by the tie of transitory existence. Shorter sketches are "The Faith of Wei Sheng,"
"Saigō Takamori," "The Garden," and "A Woman's Body."

"Absorbed in Letters" recounts the daily concerns of Takizawa
Bakin, the nineteenth-century novelist. The book depicts his
responses to criticism, his daily worries about his works-
in-progress, and finally his absorption in his creations. For a
brief moment the scene shifts to his son, who puts the whole
drama in entirely another perspective: "He is an incorrigible
fellow, isn't he?—he can't make any worthwhile money, it
seems."

As in other stories by Akutagawa, the ironies are both subtle
and profound. It would have been easy, for instance, in
"Withered Leaves," to turn the sorrowing disciples into fawning
hypocrites; instead, they are intensely human. At times
Akutagawa seems more interested in atmospheric description
than the movement of his stories, a sort of Japanese De Maupas-
sant. The translation, which leaves much to be desired, is preceded by a long introduction by John McVittie.

65. Akutagawa Ryūnosuke. *Tu Tze-Chun* [To Shi Shun]. Tr.
    by Dorothy Britton. Tokyo: Kodansha International, 1965.
    56 pp.

Tu Tze-Chun, the son of a rich man, has squandered his

inheritance and finds himself outside the gates of the city, penniless and in despair. He is saved from suicide by the sudden appearance of an old man who tells him to dig at midnight at a certain spot. Tu Tze-Chun follows the instructions and finds a coat filled with gold. Once more he wastes his money, and once more the old man leads him to wealth. Finally tiring of this pursuit of the transitory, he asks the old man to make him a wizard. The old man agrees on condition that Tu Tze-Chun not utter a word, whatever he sees or whatever is done to him. Tu Tze-Chun suffers a series of frightful trials, faithfully silent, until he witnesses the torture of his dead mother. He cries out and immediately finds himself back in everyday reality, happy at not being a wizard and content with his lot.

The story is quite short and copiously illustrated with woodcuts. Like Akutagawa's "Hell Screen," it warns against the pride that makes man reach toward superhuman attainments.

66. Yoshikawa Eiji. *The Heike Story* [Shin Heike Monogatari]. Tr. by Fuki Wooyenaka Uramatsu. New York: Alfred A. Knopf, 1958. 627 pp.

As Tanizaki Junichirō devoted much of his life to translating the *Tale of Genji* into modern Japanese, so Yoshikawa Eiji worked assiduously to reinterpret the *Tales of the Heike* (see no. **9**). The Uramatsu translation makes use of only part of Yoshikawa's work. The result is a modern, fairly omniscient and personal biography of Taira Kiyomori: his difficult, poverty-stricken youth; his rise to power through astute political maneuvering and decisive action at the right moments; and the beginning of his downfall as Minamoto Yoshitsune escapes from exile.

The novel first presents Kiyomori as an angry young man. His mother, a beautiful former mistress of the emperor, despises her husband, Tadamori. Kiyomori spends the night at a brothel with a friend, Moritō, and learns that his real father is either a rascally priest or the former emperor. Gradually the fortunes of the Heike clan begin to rise. When they are at their height, a rival clan, the Genji, stage a stunning coup, kidnapping the young emperor and the retired emperor and seizing Kyoto.

The Heike, led by Kiyomori, now a mature man, are isolated and seemingly defeated. Their leaders who are caught are beheaded along with their sons. Kiyomori, joined by allies from the provinces, however, vanquishes the Genji, and becomes the most powerful figure in the government. Acting against advice, he refuses to follow the custom of executing his enemy's young sons. Instead he sends them to monasteries to become acolytes.

After peace is restored, Kiyomori devotes himself to the development of Owada (later Kobe) as a seaport, with hopes of bringing a new renaissance to Japan by extensive cultural and economic exchange with China. By the book's end Ushiwaka, the young scion of the Genji, has escaped from his monastic retreat and plans revenge upon the Heike.

The translation is generally graceful and accurate. Since the book takes up in detail the Hōgen and Heiji wars, it provides, when combined with the Tuttle reprint of Sadler's *Tales of Heike* (in no. 14), a fine first approach to the wars of the Gen and the Hei.

67. Edogawa Rampō. *Japanese Tales of Mystery and Imagination.* Tr. by James B. Harris. Tokyo, and Rutland, Vermont: Charles E. Tuttle Co., 1956. 222 pp.

The introduction to this selection of Edogawa's stories makes clear that they have been culled from a very large body of his work. The stories all take place in a vaguely modern setting and are concerned with perpetrators of bizarre crimes, some imaginary, some real.

"The Human Chair" tells of a chairmaker isolated by his ugliness from others, and who fabricates a secret compartment in a huge chair in which to conceal himself. The chair is sold to a hotel, where the chairmaker emerges from his hiding place at opportune moments to steal valuables from the guests. The chair leads him into entanglements, since it is often occupied by a beautiful woman with whom the chairmaker falls in love.

"The Caterpillar" is a fascinating but revolting account of a man who has lost all his limbs and much of his face in battle.

He is cared for by his wife, who resents his affliction and blinds him in anger, thereby severing his last real communication with the world. Soon afterward he manages to crawl to a well and drown himself.

Other stories deal with murders. "The Psychological Test" uncovers an unsuspected murderer. "The Twins" tells, in the form of a final confession, how a man killed his twin brother and assumed his identity. "The Red Chamber" is the story of a man who allegedly murdered nearly a hundred people without exciting the least suspicion. In "Two Crippled Men" a man is made to believe he committed murder while sleepwalking.

The last story in the book, "The Traveler with the Pasted Rag Picture," concerns the supernormal. The narrator meets an old man who carries a picture portraying an old man and a strangely beautiful young woman. The aged man explains that his brother, when a young man, became hopelessly enchanted by the girl and, by the use of binoculars, managed to "enter" her portrait. Since then it has been cherished by the old man, who sadly watches the figure of his brother age.

These stories succeed as "shockers," having no pretentions to significance as literature. Although horror and violence are used for no more ambitious purpose than entertainment, they justify Edogawa's reputation as a skillful creator of suspense.

68. Osaragi Jirō [pseud. Nojiri Kiyohiko]. *Homecoming* [Kikyō]. Tr. by Brewster Horwitz. Introduction by Harold Strauss. New York: Alfred A. Knopf, 1955. 303 pp.

Kyōgo Moriya is an expatriate living in Malacca. For twenty years, he has lived without a home, but his wanderings have made him a strong and self-sufficient person. During World War II he renews acquaintance with an old friend, Ushigi, a naval captain stationed in Singapore. He is introduced by Ushigi to a lovely and mysterious woman, Saeko Takano. She involves Moriya in some illegal traffic in diamonds and when in danger betrays him, with the result that he is imprisoned until the end of the war. Everything seems changed to Moriya when he is released. He sees a dead soldier by the roadside and nearby

a bag containing salt, bearing the words: "Salt, not soiled."
This selfless offering of such a rare commodity makes Moriya
reconsider his own cynical view of humanity and he decides
to return to Japan.

Although no Americans appear in the novel, the sense of
a country defeated is conveyed through the Japanese, most of
whom seem aimless and unmotivated. Moriya is a figure of
vigorous forthrightness in the devastated country. Riding on
a train he glimpses a man who had tormented him in prison.
He follows the man and beats him. Soon afterward he learns
that his wife has remarried a pedantic professor and that his
daughter works for a fashion magazine. He has a short reunion
with his daughter, but understanding that his presence may
be embarrassing to his family, he decides to leave Japan again.
Just before his departure, Saeko arrives and apologizes for her
betrayal. He suggests a card game in which each would wager
his total possessions against the other. He wins but tells her
to give the money to a fund for the relief of war victims. With
this word he leaves to resume his wanderings.

All the characters in *Homecoming* except Kyōgo Moriya are
either devoid of will, pompous, or self-serving. In this lies the
main defect of the novel, for the author stacks the cards so
heavily in his protagonist's favor that he becomes an unbeliev-
able paragon of energy and virtue. There are, however, many
perceptive vignettes of postwar Japan. There is a short biographical sketch of Ōsaragi in the introduction.

69. Osaragi Jirō [pseud. Nojiri Kiyohiko]. *The Journey* [Tabiji].
Tr. by Ivan Morris. New York: Alfred A. Knopf, 1960.
342 pp.

This is the second of Osaragi's novels to be translated into
English. Using a pen name which means "Near the great
Buddha" (a reference to where he lives), Osaragi writes novels
strikingly similar in character depiction, theme, and setting.
They take place in postwar Japan and deal with undependable
and uneasy people in a world characterized by the erosion of
traditional values.

In *The Journey* Taeko, a young woman, visits her Uncle Soroku, an old man who has lost his son in the war. Soroku had lent his son money at interest and refuses now to aid the remaining members of his family in any financial way. Having suffered from amnesia and a failed suicide, the old man generally seems at a loss in coping with the world. In the meanwhile, his niece meets a young man named Ryosuke and the two fall in love. Ryosuke, however, proves to be both erratic in money matters and unfaithful as a lover.

The Journey, like *Homecoming*, has a variety of characters: Segi, a jovial but rather prejudiced professor, who comments on the altered world; Mrs. Iwamuro, an unscrupulous woman who panders to Americans (and is strikingly similar to Saeko of *Homecoming*); and Sutekichi, an impoverished young man who loves Taeko but cannot afford to marry her. The attempt to establish viable relationships and create some firm foundation for living fails, and the novel's conclusion finds Taeko and Ryosuke separating and old Soroku as uncertain as ever.

The Journey is an attempt to depict a relatively large cast of characters, all of whom reflect the malaise of their time and country, but the novel fails to reach any meaningful depth of insight. It is historically significant, nevertheless, as one of the first Japanese novels published in America after the war.

70. Nakagawa Yoichi. *A Moonflower in Heaven* [Ten no Yugao]. Tr. by Ōta Akira. Tokyo: Hokuseido Press, 1949. 96 pp.

This plaintive tale of a passionate, unfulfilled love might be compared to Goethe's *The Sorrows of Young Werther* and Constant's *Adolphe* in Western literature. The narrator of *A Moonflower in Heaven* says, "I wagered my life on one dream." As a student at the university in Kyoto, he meets a young married woman, Akiko-san, whose mother has just died. In this atmosphere of sadness the two become attracted to one another. Their respective obligations make it impossible for them to express their love, and they can meet only infrequently. While they are apart the narrator can think of little but his absent love and longs for the time when they will have a few moments together.

The anguish of separation drives the narrator to strange behavior. In preparation for a hermit's life in the snowy mountains, he pitches a tent in the suburbs. Then he sets out for the mountains, where he finds a remote spot to live bereft of companionship and learns the songs of the birds. Winter comes, and his life becomes "more and more lonely, with something like madness added to it." Still, he is constantly haunted by thoughts of his absent love. In the spring he leaves his retreat and comes down into the lowlands to search for Akiko. By the time he finds her, many years have passed and she is older. "But to me it was a matter of no importance. I had already ceased to love her youth."

After this last meeting she dies. Their unrequited love has lasted over twenty years, but he continues to assert his undying love for her and communicates with her through fireworks, "those evanescent summer-night sparks, shooting towards the heavens where she is."

The monomaniacal passion of the narrator and his unremitting pursuit more of the idea of his beloved than her reality are movingly told in this short novel. But it is difficult for the occidental reader to accept this genre—the romantic short novel—a form that has been extinct in Western literature for almost a century and a half.

71.   Ibuse Masuji. *Black Rain* [Kuroi Ame]. Tr. by John Bester. Tokyo, and Palo Alto, California: Kodansha International, 1969. 300 pp.

Japanese literature since World War II has produced numerous accounts of the Hiroshima atomic holocaust, and a number have appeared in English. *Black Rain* is clearly the best. It takes place some years after the war's end and deals with Shigematsu Shizuma's concern for his niece Yasuko, who cannot find a suitor because she had been working near Hiroshima on that fateful day, and the inhabitants of the village where they now live, some hundred miles away from Hiroshima, fear she is a victim of radiation sickness. Several promising marriage possibilities have not materialized as a result.

Shigematsu spends much of his time recopying the diary he wrote during those terrible days at Hiroshima, and the novel alternates between the quiet serenity of the present and the terrifying past of the diary. Shigematsu remembers grotesque incidents, such as the behavior of a woman buried in rubble who threw tiles at those trying to rescue her. While escaping the city with his wife, all around them were horribly charred corpses, people wandering aimlessly about with ghastly burns, and strange rumors about a bomb filled with poison gas. Medical supplies and personnel were grossly inadequate, and the bureaucratic ineptitude of the military compounded the terror.

Those who survived often found that their hair and teeth fell out, and many were to die soon. Shigematsu himself was very ill and survived for a long time on a diet of pears. Although Yasuko showed no signs of illness, during the course of the novel symptoms appear which are clearly those of radiation poisoning, indicating her impending death.

Black Rain is not *the* great novel about the bombing of Hiroshima, but it is a moving work. Although the factual account of horror upon horror is often diverted by the absurdity and grotesqueness of various incidents, *Black Rain* achieves much of its power through the author's careful recital of detail after detail, which builds to a tremendous crescendo.

72. Kawabata Yasunari. *Snow Country* [Yukiguni]. Tr. by Edward Seidensticker. New York: Alfred A. Knopf, 1956. 175 pp. (Paperback, Berkley Medallion Books).

73. ———. *Thousand Cranes* [Senbazuru]. Tr. by Edward Seidensticker. New York: Alfred A. Knopf, 1958. 147 pp. (Paperback, Berkley Medallion Books).

On the basis of these two short novels (available in a single volume from Knopf, 1969) the Nobel Prize committee chose to award Kawabata the 1968 Prize for Literature. The choice surprised even the Japanese, who had long admired Kawabata but felt his work was not understood in the West.

Kawabata's themes are fairly restricted. Central to them is

analysis and an implied reproof of the motives of the sensitive, sexually aggressive artists familiar in the I-novels, and sometimes, but not always, suggesting Kawabata himself. In *Snow Country* he gives us Shimamura—literally, "island village" —who seems only to live with his wife and children in Tokyo, occasionally visiting a certain hot spring resort on Japan's snowy seacoast. Shimamura seems most concerned with enjoying, when he pleases, the volatile intimacies of Komako, a country geisha, and meditating about the enigmatic beauty of Yōko, a girl younger than Komako, with whom Komako lives. In *Thousand Cranes* Kawabata's persona is Kikuji Mitani (surname, literally "three valleys"), son of a man who loved the tea ceremony and, by turns, at least three women. Kikuji's concern is to find a loving wife not connected with his dead father. In this he fails repeatedly.

Upon this spare canvas all of the concentrated effort of Kawabata is expended. In many ways he resembles Henry James—in the delicacy of his presentation and his analysis of human motives in circumstances of complex social interaction. Unlike James, however, Kawabata's style is simple. His sentences and paragraphs are staccato and incrementally repetitive. In the introduction to the combined volume, Edward Seidensticker compares Kawabata's style to that of haiku. Indeed, the translation sensitively presents statement after statement resembling a string of haiku, as does this passage from the chapter of *Thousand Cranes* entitled "Her Mother's Lipstick":

It was a plain indigo morning glory, probably wild, and most ordinary. The vine was thin, and the leaves and blossom were small.

But the green and the deep blue were cool, falling over a red-lacquered gourd dark with age.

The maid, who had been with the family from his father's time, was imaginative in her way.

On the gourd was a fading lacquer seal-signature, and on its ancient-looking box the mark of the first owner, Sōtan, which, if authentic, would make it three hundred years old.

Kikuji knew nothing about tea flowers, nor was the maid likely to be well-informed. For morning tea, however, it seemed to him that the morning glory was most appropriate.

He gazed at it for a time. In a gourd that had been handed down for three centuries, a flower that would fade in a morning.

Kawabata's style has also been compared with that of the *renga*, or linked verse, which is made up of stanzas alternating in syllable counts of seventeen and fourteen. As each stanza is composed, the three or more poets writing the poem judge it as to how well it combines with the preceding stanza. The above excerpt demonstrates how the techniques of *renga* might be adapted to prose, with key words repeated many times in spite of close coherence between paragraphs so that old elements form new and exciting combinations.

In *Snow Country* the elements are snow scenes that the Japanese associate with mountain resorts near the Japan Sea and their hot spring hotel atmosphere they enjoy whenever possible, the pathos of the geisha Komako's work and her tangled personal life, and the mysterious beauty of her ward Yōko. Shimamura interacts with these elements in separate isolated intervals, irregularly spaced over a period of a few years, doing nothing to help Komako and Yōko. He actually aggravates their problems, which is the unstated theme of this sad and all too real novel.

In *Thousand Cranes* the essential elements are the tea ceremony, including its tools, its mystique, its practitioners, its matchmaking functions, and, as Kawabata himself said in his Nobel Prize acceptance speech, its decay. There is a birthmark, on Chikako's breast (one of the protagonist's dead father's mistresses), something Kikuji saw when a child, and which still haunts him and the life he wishes to fashion for himself like a black, spirit-sucking beast out of an old *monogatari*. Finally, there is the thousand-crane motif on the *furoshiki* or carrying cloth (the translation "kerchief" misleads), in which the lovely Inamura girl carries her tea-ceremony necessities as the book opens. That motif is not alluded to after the very beginning of the book, but it continues to symbolize the beautiful, clean, free world Kikuji would like to reside in.

The complicated lives, past and present, of the young man and four women weave and interweave. Kikuji, drawn to the Inamura girl, attempts to avoid the influence of the birthmarked Chikako who has brought them together. He soon becomes involved with another of his father's mistresses, with whom he is intimate in scenes weighted with oedipal significance.

Finally, after the mistress's suicide, he becomes involved with her daughter, Fumiko. At the novel's end, the reader is left with the enigma of Kikuji's future. Has he exorcised his father's ghost? Can he leave his ancestral house, the tea house behind it, the priceless tea utensils left by his father? And can he free himself from the more recent events in his life and move into some thousand-crane world that is his human birthright? Kawabata does not answer such questions; his genius lies in posing them.

74. Kawabata Yasunari. *House of the Sleeping Beauties and Other Stories* [Nemureru Bijo]. Tr. by Edward G. Seidensticker. Tokyo and Palo Alto: Kodansha International, 1969. 149 pp. (Paperback, Ballantine Books).

The title story of this volume is strikingly reminiscent of some of Tanizaki's short fiction, particularly "A Portrait of Shunkin" and "The Bridge of Dreams." An old man, Eguchi, is the patron of a strange house where aged men come to sleep with beautiful and drugged girls. The primary rule of the establishment is that the girls must not be violated. Unlike most of the patrons, Eguchi is not impotent. The silent, sleeping girls arouse him and, as he lies beside one after another, he recalls uncomfortably his own daughters as well as the numerous affairs of his past. His mood is serene and meditative, this strange house like a gatehouse to paradise.

"One Arm" is a fantasy about a man's possession of only that portion of a girl's anatomy. "Of Birds and Beasts" tells of a man whose pets all die. The implication is that his relations with people are similar. All three stories explore the sensibility of a man who essentially rejects the humanity of things—for they are turned into just that—that feed his sensuousness.

The title story is a masterpiece of reflection, controlled ambiguity, and suggestive reverberation. The depth of this story forcefully implies that the occidental world has not yet begun to understand eroticism, the most complex and compelling theme conceivable in literature.

75. Kawabata Yasunari. *The Sound of the Mountain* [Yama no Oto]. Tr. by Edward Seidensticker. New York: Alfred A. Knopf, 1970. 276 pp. (Paperback, Berkley Medallion Books).

This, the most recent Kawabata novel to appear in English, shares with *House of the Sleeping Beauties* a concern for the sensuality in the aging man and with *Snow Country* and *Thousand Cranes* deep sympathy for women tormented by male infidelity. Shingo, in his sixties, presides uncertainly over a family whose marriages have all failed in one way or another. He has lost all feeling for his wife, and they live together only as partakers of meaningless, shared rituals. The son has neglected his wife for a mistress (both are pregnant, but it is the wife who plans to have an abortion). Shingo's daughter has left her husband and returned to her parents with her two children. Although he tries to help his offspring, Shingo finds himself drawn back into the pangs and temptations of sensuality—even while there is deep human understanding—through the closeness of his son's wife.

Kawabata's allusiveness and subtlety are as pervasive here as in his other novels, but *The Sound of the Mountain* lacks the direct sexual involvements of *Snow Country, Thousand Cranes,* or even *House of the Sleeping Beauties.*

76. Sugimoto, Etsu Inagaki. *A Daughter of the Samurai.* Tokyo, and Rutland, Vermont: Charles E. Tuttle Co., 1966. 314 pp.

A Daughter of the Samurai is the reissue of a book first published in 1926, and often referred to in Ruth Benedict's classic study of the Japanese character, *The Chrysanthemum and the Sword.* It is the autobiography of a woman of the samurai clan who, after experiencing a traditional Japanese childhood, is married to a young Japanese who has emigrated to the United States. She joins him there, bears him two daughters, is widowed, and returns to Japan. The book closes with her preparations to return to her husband's family in America.

Sugimoto is not a sociologist, but has a fine eye for discerning
the customs of two radically different lands and a skillful way
of making the reader feel some of the cultural shock experienced
in her transition from one society to another. She recounts her
rigid training as the daughter of an influential samurai. Her
father's courage during civil disturbances and her mother's
unruffled stoicism when the life of her husband and son were
threatened instructed her in the virtues of calm acceptance. She
records her immense difficulties in adjusting to America and
her eldest daughter's readjustment when they return to Japan.

A Daughter of the Samurai is unique in its understanding
of two vastly different cultures, and makes no judgments as
to the superiority of either. Published over forty years ago,
it is of great importance in the history of American-Japanese
understanding. Delicate, sensitive, restrained, it may have
unwittingly contributed to the assumption, prior to World War
II, that the Japanese were too peaceful and artistic to wage an
aggressive war.

77. Sugimoto, Etsu Inagaki. *A Daughter of the Narikin.* Garden
    City, New York: Doubleday, Doran & Co., 1932. 325 pp.
78. ———. *A Daughter of the Nohfu.* Garden City, New York:
    Doubleday, Doran & Co., 1935. 340 pp.

A Daughter of the Narikin (*narikin* meaning nouveau riche)
is important mostly as one of the earliest fictional introductions
of modern Japan to a large Western audience. It can be especially
recommended to grade- and high-school students.

A Daughter of the Nohfu (*nohfu* meaning farmer or peasant)
is a more carefully wrought and more unified novel than *A
Daughter of the Narikin.* It can be recommended to anyone who
wants to understand Japanese village life in the years before
World War II.

79. Kobayashi Takiji. *The Cannery Boat and Other Japanese Short
    Stories* [Kani Kōsen]. No translator listed. (1933). Westport,
    Connecticut: Greenwood Press, 1968. 271 pp.

This reissue of a volume first published in 1933 by International Publishers includes only a portion of *The Cannery Boat* and summarizes the remainder. The stories, all concerned with social justice, are didactically Marxist in theme.

The Cannery Boat tells of a group of impoverished workers and students who sign up on a ship to catch and can crabs. The work is tedious and exhausting, the bosses brutal. The workers are very poorly fed, and some contract diseases. When one of the smaller boats loses contact with the mother ship it strays to the Russian coast where the workers have a chance to meet and talk with some happy communists and contrast their sad lot with that of those in the worker's state.

There are numerous examples of the suppression of all human values in order to get the crabs canned most efficiently. When a ship not far away sends a distress signal, the crab-canning ship ignores it. The ship in trouble sinks and several hundred lives are lost. The last portion of the novel tells of a protest strike that fails. *The Cannery Boat* is the best-known example of the proletarian school of writing that came to fruition in the late twenties.

The stories that accompany the novel are similar in theme. "Linesman" [*sic*] tells of bad conditions among the telephone linemen. "Lieutenant Kusama" is the story of a young army officer who becomes indignant at social injustice. "The Efficiency Committee" recounts the efforts of factory owners to break a strike.

The works in this volume have limited literary value, although there are some moving passages in *The Cannery Boat*. The propagandistic effect of the stories was obviously foremost in the intent of the compilers.

80. Takeyama Michio. *Harp of Burma* [Biruma no Tategoto]. Tr. by Howard Hibbett. Tokyo, Japan: Charles E. Tuttle Co., 1966. 132 pp.

Harp of Burma, a lyrical, affirmative novel about man's capacity to transcend the horror of war, takes place in Burma during

and after the final days of World War II. The narrator, one
of a group of Japanese soldiers who was repatriated after the
war, recounts the experiences of his unit in the last days of
the war, telling how they entered a Burmese village and were
welcomed heartily and feasted by the people there. After the
celebration they receive word that they are about to be attacked
by the British, and in order to reach their weapons stacked
in the village, they must pretend to be unaware of this imminent
attack. They feign obliviousness to their danger by singing
—among the songs is one to the tune of "Home Sweet Home."
The British soldiers join in the song, the battle is forestalled,
and the Japanese are informed that the war is over.

One of their company, Mizushima, a skillful harp player and
chorus leader, volunteers to go with the British to attempt to
persuade a fanatical group of Japanese soldiers to surrender,
now that hostilities have ended. Despite his dedicated efforts,
he is unsuccessful, and as a result becomes separated from his
company. Some months later, the members of his original company, now interned and awaiting repatriation, see a strange
Buddhist monk wandering about near their compound. Before
embarkation, the monk reveals himself as Mizushima, and
leaves a letter relating that he must remain in Burma to bury
the dead Japanese whose bones dot the countryside, and to
make amends for his country's bloody war of territorial con-
quest.

This simple, gracefully translated poetic novel, suited for the
young as well as the mature reader, is a striking contrast to
most war novels. Although the horrors of war may appear to
some to be smoothed over, its brevity is sufficient excuse for
its intense dedication to the idea of humanity triumphing over
its capacity for greed and destruction.

81. Niwa Fumio. *The Buddha Tree* [Bodai Ju]. Tr. by Kenneth
    Strong. London: Peter Owen, 1966. 380 pp. (Paperback,
    Charles E. Tuttle Co.).

The Buddha Tree is a long, intense novel by a prolific novelist
of postwar life in Japan. The main character, Soshu, is a priest
of the True Pure Land sect of Buddhism, who has achieved

his honored position through adoption into the family of the priest of Butsuoji. The novel is a painstaking portrayal of everyday life in this provincial hamlet, showing the forces at work in the modern secular world that gradually erode much of the impact that Buddhism formerly had on the lives of its practitioners.

Soshu had been adopted into the Getsudo family because his prospective mother-in-law, Mineyo, then still a relatively young woman, was in love with him. Although he is legally married to her daughter, Renko, and has a son, Ryokun, he nonetheless continues an affair of many years with Mineyo. His wife, neglected by her husband and abused by her mother, goes off with a kabuki actor and later becomes the wife of a village headman.

Much of the novel is concerned with Soshu's inner torment. His genuine religious inclinations are sullied by his unsavory liaison with Mineyo, and his sense of guilt becomes so great after his wife leaves that he determines to break relations with his demanding mother-in-law. His son, Ryokun, feels desolate without his mother, and vaguely senses the tensions at home.

The one thing of beauty in Soshu's life is Tomoko, a widow who, in order to support her daughter, has become the mistress of a wealthy local businessman. Tomoko is repelled by her patron's brutal lovemaking and reciprocates Shoshu's love. At the end of the novel, Soshu confesses his illicit relations with Mineyo before his congregation and plans to leave Butsuoji, while Tomoko tries but finds it impossible to leave her patron.

The Buddha Tree is unusual among Japanese novels. Its minute depiction of the ordinary round of existence—particularly that of a Buddhist priest—makes it almost seem a realistic novel in the Western sense. Movingly and skillfully narrated, it may strike the occidental reader as having insufficient focus. It is hard to say whether it is essentially the story of Soshu, Ryokun, or Tomoko. But there is certainly no Japanese novel in translation that offers such a loving, compassionate picture of village life in modern Japan.

82. Hayashi Fumiko. *Floating Cloud* [Ukigumo]. Tr. by Y. Koitabashi. Tokyo: Information Publishing Co., 1957. 110 pp.

This translation of a novel first published in 1953 deals primarily with the effects of postwar society on two Japanese lovers. Yukiko, a young woman with no permanent attachments, has a number of affairs, in which she is usually made the loser. To escape a difficult situation she goes to Indochina, then occupied by the Japanese, where she meets the man who is to figure largest in her life, Tomioka. He is married but clearly no longer loves his wife.

After the surrender they return to Japan separately to face the awful problems of their devastated and occupied country. Yukiko lives for a time with an American soldier, managing to sustain a rudimentary existence by working at various menial jobs. The sense of foreboding created in the earlier part of the novel then changes to an atmosphere of gloom and despair. Yukiko persists in her drab life, clinging to the hope that somehow she will be reunited with Tomioka now torn between her and other women.

Yukiko becomes pregnant by her lover but seeks an abortion because he is infatuated with a younger and more attractive girl. At the same time the object of Tomioka's affections is killed by her jealous employer. Tomioka takes a job as a forestry expert, and he and Yukiko leave the city for an island where he is to assume his new work. However, Yukiko dies and their hopes for a happy life together are unrealized.

This inconclusive novel is a sensitive and probing study of rootless people (floating clouds) whose personal difficulties are reflected in the aimless and sad existence of people made spiritually homeless by war. The story is told without sentimentality or vicarious self-pity. The translation, unfortunately, shows a poor grasp of the English idiom and is, at times, both unclear and ungrammatical.

83. Ishikawa Tatsuzō. *Resistance at Forty-Eight* [Shijūhassai no Teikō]. Tr. by Nakayama Kazuma. Tokyo: Hokuseido Press, 1960. 343 pp.

Resistance at Forty-Eight is an account of the inner life of Kotaro Nishimura, an official in an insurance company who is depressed by approaching middle age. Although fond of his wife and devoted to his daughter, his life is empty and unfulfilled. Nishimura buys a copy of Goethe's *Faust* at a bookstore and sees Faust in himself—a dissatisfied man who devoted his life to a profession that failed to satisfy him. The rest of the novel parallels Nishimura's experience with that of Faust.

A younger employee of the insurance company, Hosuke Soga, plays the part of Nishimura's Mephistopheles, introducing him to pornographic photography. Nishimura is immediately enchanted by the beautiful young girl he sees surrounded by eager men snapping pictures, and she becomes Nishimura's fantasy Gretchen. While he tries to deal with his infatuation for her, he is confronted with his daughter's rebellion. She has run off with a man younger than she, far from an ideal son-in-law.

Soga arranges for Nishimura to spend the weekend with the object of his love, which proves a fiasco. Nishimura is tempted to take bribes to support a mistress, but in the end he returns to his wife, resigned both to the unsuitability of his daughter's marriage and the futility of resisting it.

Resistance at Forty-Eight is a skillful yet modest treatment of a familiar theme in modern literature: the rebellion of the unfulfilled man. Ishikawa forgoes the sensational and the melodramatic in his account of his protagonist's abortive rebellion, instead leaving him with sad discontent with the routine of ordinary life. The translation falls short of normal standards of publication in English.

84. Inoue Yasushi. *The Hunting Gun* [Ryōjū]. Tr. by Sadamichi Yokoo and Sanford Goldstein. Rutland, Vermont, and Tokyo: Charles E. Tuttle Co., 1961. 74 pp.

This short novel, first published in 1959, was partially responsible for Inoue's receipt of the Akutagawa Prize in 1960. It is a subtle, probing work, narrated by an outsider who chances on something that opens a door into the life of another. The narrator writes a poem about a hunter and receives a response from a man who insists he is the poem's subject. This man, Josuke Misugi, encloses letters from three different women, each of whom has a different relationship to the recipient. The first comes from the daughter of a woman with whom Josuke has had an affair. The second is from Josuke's wife, who recalls the first days of her marriage and her gradual disillusionment with her husband. The final letter is from Josuke's mistress, written just before her suicide.

The first letter is the simplest; it tells of the daughter's shock at discovering her mother's guilt, and how this knowledge brought her into the sad realm of maturity. The wife speaks in the second letter of her growing but indefinable estrangement from Josuke, and asks, "When you could shoot a pheasant or a turtledove with your hunting gun, why couldn't you shoot me through the heart? If you deceived me at all, why didn't you deceive me more cruelly, more thoroughly?" The third and final letter from the mistress seems to offer a justification for the sufferings of the others, but it is inconclusive. Josuke has failed all three of these women, but he has failed them in different ways. The portrait each creates of Josuke is so intensely personal that the man himself eludes final description. Each of the women has been disappointed because the man she has reached out to is primarily the creation of her illusion. All four characters, their dreams shattered, are left in isolation.

The Hunting Gun is a masterful work, verbal reflecting mirrors in which no answers are final and no motive is certain. It refuses to compromise the complexity of life by offering simple answers and expresses the fact that truth is as difficult as the process of attaining it.

85.   Inoue Yasushi. *The Counterfeiter and Other Stories*. Tr. by Leon Picon. Rutland, Vermont, and Tokyo: Charles E. Tuttle Co., 1965. 124 pp.

A collection of three stories by the author of *The Hunting Gun*, these stories, like that work, are concerned with identity, loneliness, and the difficulty of relating to others. "The Counterfeiter" is narrated by an art critic who has undertaken to write the biography of Keigaku, a recently deceased painter of some note. Since Keigaku was a rather elusive person whom no one seems to have known well, the prospective biographer searches out one person who is mentioned several times in Keigaku's diary. This man, Hosen, is revealed as the capable forger of works sold as Keigaku's. But the paintings are not common forgeries, and possess a strange integrity of their own. As one character says: "For eyes that had just witnessed so many Keigaku masterpieces, this painting of course could not compete, but yet there was a spirit of destitution and solitude which had disciplined the work."

Intrigued by this strange forger, the narrator traces his life to his death in a remote village. In the last years the old man gave up painting and made fireworks in the hope, despite repeated failure, of producing a flame of a special deep blue violet. His whole life turned out to be a series of attempts to reach impossible goals; his forgeries were not mere unscrupulous commercial ventures but sincere attempts to attain an unattainable level of excellence.

The other two stories are less impressive. "Obasute" is a mountain where, it is said, familes used to abandon old people. The narrator is strangely attracted to the area because of its reputation as a fine place for moon-viewing, and also because it seems to symbolize an escape from the difficulties of human relationships. He travels to Mount Obasute, decides that the "fall colors seem better than the moon" and, in that observation, asserts his preference for life over the prospect of isolation that the mountain offers. The final story, "The Full Moon," is a short narrative of a man's rise and fall in a large corporation.

Inoue is a writer engrossed by the ambiguities of the human soul. These satires, like *The Hunting Gun*, evince a fascination with the unexpected and the unpredictable. Much of their power comes from Inoue's unwillingness to resolve the complexities he has uncovered. The most he will venture is what the narrator discovers at the end of "The Counterfeiter": "Eternity was something related to Keigaku and Hosen, and yet, ironically, life held one small reality which was irrelevant to both. . . . "

86. Hino Ashihei [pseud. Tamai Katsunori]. *War and Soldier.* Tr. by Lewis Bush. London: Putnam, 1940. 579 pp.

War and Soldier, divided into four parts, is a composite rendering of a number of Hino's books, their titles all ending in "... and Soldier" (... *to Heitai*): "Mud and Soldier," "Flower and Soldier," "Wheat and Soldier" (most familiar to the American reader through Donald Keene's selection in *Modern Japanese Literature*, no. **114**), and "Sea and Soldier." They form a Japanese Ernie Pyle's account of the Japanese invasion of China in the years previous to America's entry into World War II. The fighting takes place near the coast of China, around Hangchow and Shanghai and later near Hongkong, between 1937 and 1938.

There is no attempt in any of the sections to minimize the horror of war. A baby held by its dead mother is described with great sympathy, as are the wounded and dead soldiers of both sides. The author is moved and angered by the plight of a Chinese soldier chained by his superiors to his machine gun in a pillbox. Most of Hino's sentiments are predictably chauvinistic, and at no time does he question the justice of Japan's cause or the necessity of war. Chinese civilians are invariably shown welcoming the invading hosts, although at times their sincerity is suspect.

Hino graphically and skillfully describes a series of military incursions. In spite of their vividness the quality of the book cannot compare with a work like Henri Barbusse's *Under Fire*. The author's responses are conventional and he was obviously wary of censorship.

87. Dazai Osamu. *The Setting Sun* [Shayō]. Tr. by Donald Keene. New York: New Directions, 1956. 175 pp. (Paperback).

The Setting Sun depicts the decline of the Japanese aristocracy in the years following World War II. The narrator, a mature woman named Kazuko, has come with her mother to the country, since their financial difficulties prevent their maintaining the big family house in Tokyo. The mother is a true aristocrat of the old world, with a clear view of life's proprieties, while her daughter, divorced by her husband, believes in nothing. Her brother, Naoji, is a drug addict, and offers no prospect for reviving the family fortunes.

Kazuko and her mother are clearly incapable of coping with life as it has become. Kazuko tries, unsuccessfully, to work in the fields to raise food; and she almost sets the house afire accidentally. She writes long letters to Uehara, an artist who hopes to find what little meaning life holds for him in dissolution. Although she loves Uehara, he is married and can offer no promise of a permanent relationship. The mother becomes increasingly ill and Naoji, despairing of his life, finally commits suicide. He leaves behind a testament in which he says, "I am better off dead. I haven't the capacity to stay alive. I haven't the strength to quarrel with people over money. I can't even touch people for a hand-out." Kazuko goes to Uehara and they have a child, the only ray of hope in the novel.

Dazai's handling of his three major characters is skillful. Kazuko as narrator stands between her brother, who furnishes the philosophical explanation of the family malaise, and her mother, who cannot adjust to radically changed conditions. The three form a continuum of growing alienation, and it is Kazuko and her child who offer the only prospect for survival. Naoji's thoughts are reproduced largely from his notebooks and random writings, giving Kazuko's experiences another dimension of meaning.

The Western reader is likely to feel he has been through all this before. Baudelaire and Dostoyevsky have handled the corruption of the self with more artistry and profundity. But the setting here is new and the agonized portrayal of these people forced to cope with drastic change makes this a moving, if somewhat derivative, novel.

88. Dazai Osamu. *No Longer Human* [Ningen Shikkaku]. Tr. by Donald Keene. New York: New Directions, 1958. 177 pp. (Paperback).

Some of the same territory of human degradation depicted in Dazai's *The Setting Sun* is explored here. The narrator acquires some notebooks describing the life and dissipations of Yōzō, the protagonist. Aside from the short opening and closing chapters, the whole of the novel consists of Yōzō's self-examination in the notebooks. The work is very reminiscent in its self-laceration of Dostoyevsky's *Notes from the Underground*.

One of Yōzō's first discoveries as a child is that the view that others have of him does not correspond to the self he knows. This puzzles and annoys him, and he protects himself by playing roles, usually comic ones. His impersonations are successful but he knows instinctively the self others love is not the real Yōzō. He cannot reciprocate their approbation. He comes to understand society as "the struggle between one individual and another, a then-and-there struggle in which immediate triumph is everything. *Human beings never submit to human beings.*"

Yōzō's closest friend is Horoki, a companion in his seamy escapades. Yōzō lives with a number of different women, falling more and more into a life of dissipation. Soon, unable to maintain even a marginal existence, he begins taking drugs and becomes an addict (like Naoji of *The Setting Sun*). The end of the novel finds him in a lunatic asylum.

No Longer Human is not as impressive as *The Setting Sun*. Unlike that novel, it explores just one aspect of degradation, and Yōzō's experience is only slightly related to the social reality of the world around him. But the work does evince a penetrating honesty and ruthless self-examination. Yōzō does not blink, faced even by the most horrible visions of his personal hell.

89. Ōoka Shōhei. *Fires on the Plain* [Nobi]. Tr. by Ivan Morris. New York: Alfred A. Knopf, 1957. 246 pp. (Paperback, Penguin Books).

Most war novels focus upon the horrors of war as realized in the direct encounters of the military forces. *Fires on the Plain*, concerned little with the front lines, is an exception. John Bayley, writing in *The Spectator*, spoke of it as "a more impressive novel about the war than any I have come across from England or America."

The novel is narrated in the first person by Private Tamura, a tubercular Japanese soldier who, along with a number of others, is refused treatment in the field hospital. The scene is the Philippines when the Americans were recapturing those islands. Tamura becomes separated from his company and wanders, starving, about the countryside. Strangely attracted by a church in a deserted village, he enters and is moved by the religious paintings on the walls. Here, partly in confusion, he kills a woman. Plagued by guilt, he continues to wander, seeing everywhere the nauseous rotting bodies of his fellow soldiers —described in graphic detail—and evidence of cannibalism. From the time of the visit to the church, the novel is suffused with Christian imagery. But even if one realizes that the author is Roman Catholic, it is by no means clear how these images are to be interpreted.

At the point of death, Private Tamura is saved from starvation by a fellow soldier. He stays with this comrade and another soldier, gradually realizing that they are subsisting on human flesh, not monkey meat as they had claimed. Unable to face the insupportable horror of what he has witnessed, Tamura insists that life is only bearable if he can be transformed.

I was seized with anger: if as a result of hunger human beings were constrained to eat each other, then this world of ours was no more than the result of God's wrath. And if I at this moment could vomit forth anger, then I, who was no longer human, must be an angel of God, and an instrument of God's wrath.

Impelled by this thought, he kills his companion. The epilogue, entitled "A Madman's Diary," describes Tamura's life in a mental institution after the war. He performs a ritual of propitiation, asking forgiveness, before eating any organic matter, and he tries to comprehend the meaning of his experience in the war. However, the ultimate answers remain unclear.

A number of Western reviewers have interpreted this novel as a story of a man's conversion to Christianity. This is highly questionable. The Christian imagery is possibly used only for artistic effect. *Fire on the Plains* is complex and difficult, conceived with a manic intensity that may someday earn it recognition as a masterpiece.

90. Shiina Rinzō. *The Flowers are Fallen* [Ai no Shogen]. Tr. by Sydney Giffard. London: Heinemann, 1961. 208 pp.

Seiko Nakada is a sensitive working girl of eighteen who

lives with her parents and a somewhat disreputable uncle,
Nobuo, a movie comedian who later confesses his love for her.
Seiko, shocked by the suicide of a close friend, feels nonetheless
that this friend has triumphed in not allowing herself to be
tainted by the world.

At her work Seiko especially dislikes the head clerk, Yamada,
who makes casually cruel advances to her. Seiko wants above
all to live purely, uncompromised by the sordid realities of
life personified by Yamada. She goes on several errands for
Yamada, only to discover, after a number of her fellow workers
are laid off, that she has unknowingly participated in their dis-
charge. Angered and humiliated, she resolves, in the end, to
face the "many new and entirely different troubles waiting for
her."

The Flowers are Fallen is short, unpretentious, and not wholly
convincing. Seiko's difficulties are described with compassion
and insight, but Shiina has not penetrated deeply enough into
her character to enable the reader to feel the depth of her revulsion toward life.

91. Takeda Taijun. *This Outcast Generation and Luminous Moss.*
Tr. by Shibuya Yusaburo and Sanford Goldstein. Rutland,
Vermont, and Tokyo: Charles E. Tuttle Co., 1967. 145 pp.

Both of these stories deal with the price of man's survival
in terms of the death of others. Sugi, the narrator of *This Outcast
Generation* [Mamushi no Sue] lives in Shanghai after World War
II, making his living translating important documents into Chinese for his desperate compatriots. He reflects sardonically that
he is existing off the misery of others.

A woman comes to Sugi for help, confessing that she is married to an invalid who is not expected to recover, and has reluctantly become the mistress of Karajima, formerly a Japanese
official and now, quite probably, a war criminal. Sugi, overwhelmed by the woman's beauty, agrees to help her and her
husband escape to Japan. The husband welcomes Sugi's aid,
but is wary of Sugi's feelings toward his wife. Later, Karajima
is killed and Sugi and the woman leave Shanghai together with
the woman's husband at the point of death.

Luminous Moss [Hikari Goke] begins as the narrative of a journey to the north of Japan but becomes a play. The narrator has stumbled upon some of the famous and long-sought "luminous moss." This discovery leads him to ponder on instances of one form of life feeding on another, in response to which his guide tells him of a famous case of cannibalism, in which the captain of a wrecked ship ate the members of his crew. The narrator then imagines a play in two acts. In the first, the captain and his crew are brutal men feeding on one another like animals. In the second act, the captain—who according to the stage directions should be played by another, more subtle actor—quietly explains that his horrible act was necessary for survival. The play closes with the captain asking the members of the court to look closely and observe the ring of light—his luminous sign of guilt—around his neck. They look, and rings of light appear about their own necks.

These short works are two of the most impressive works of prose to appear in Japanese literature since the war. Takeda's humanism, wholly unsentimental, takes into account the terrible sufferings men must inflict upon each other to survive, and emphasizes the guilt of all. The translation is both accurate and graceful.

92. Noma Hiroshi. *Zone of Emptiness* [Shinkū Chitai]. Tr. from the French by Bernard Frechtman. Cleveland and New York: World Publishing Co., 1958. 317 pp.

Zone of Emptiness is a story of the Japanese army in the final days of World War II. Yet it is not, strictly speaking, a war novel. The scene is an army camp where most of the battles are private struggles between individual men. The main character, Kitani, is a disgruntled soldier who has been treated badly by life. Army life is shown to be brutal, confining, and mindless, as noted by Kitani in his diary.

A series of flashbacks reveals how Kitani was accused of stealing the wallet of Lieutenant Hayashi and sentenced to a harsh military prison. In reality Kitani had only found the wallet by chance, but he was charged with theft, court-martialed, and

treated cruelly because of the entries in his diary that criticized
the inhuman treatment that is part of the soldier's life.

Another soldier equally unhappy with the army is Soda, an
intellectual, who befriends Kitani. Soda gives another, almost
philosophical, dimension to Kitani's just grievances. At the end
of the novel, Lieutenant Hayashi is transferred to Kitani's company. Kitani's smoldering desire for revenge finds an outlet.
He confronts his accuser, discovers he had been unjustly sentenced, and beats the lieutenant brutally. After this incident
he is selected for front-line duty and goes off to certain death.

Although graphic in its evocation of the horror of an ignorant,
brutalizing hierarchy, *Zone of Emptiness* is also at times tedious,
and it depends too much on repetition for its effects. It is,
nevertheless, a worthwhile complement to *Fires on the Plain*
(no. **89**) and *Harp of Burma* (no. **80**), both of which deal also
with the effect of war, directly or indirectly, on human beings.
Noma is an avowed Marxist, and Kitani and Soda are obviously
meant to represent the worker and the intellectual as victims
of an imperialistic government.

The novel was originally translated from the Japanese into
French, and then into English. The prose does not always read
smoothly.

93. Agawa Hiroyuki. *Devil's Heritage* [Ma no Isan]. Tr. by John
M. Maki. Tokyo: Hokuseido Press, 1957. 247 pp.

Devil's Heritage might best be described as a documentary
novel. Its protagonist, Sankichi Noguchi, visits Hiroshima to
gather material for a literary report to be entitled "Hiroshima
Eight Years After the Atomic Bomb." One of his first stops
is at the Atomic Bomb Casualty Commission (ABCC), a research
organization set up by the Americans immediately after Japan's
surrender to investigate the effects of the nuclear explosion upon
the residents of Hiroshima and offer some measure of treatment.

Noguchi visits his uncle, whose young son has developed
what proves later to be leukemia. Noguchi discovers, during
the course of his interviews, that the ABCC is widely distrusted
by the inhabitants of Hiroshima, who see it as an extremely

secretive organization concerned only with gathering information for Americans and officially unwilling to admit that the marked incidence of leukemia in Hiroshima can be in any way related to the atomic bomb. Noguchi talks with a large number of people who suffered from the catastrophe, including members of the Willow Society—a group of people who have been in various ways injured and deformed as a result of the blast. At the novel's end, the uncle's son dies, his autopsy described in excruciating detail.

The novel is actually a series of frighteningly effective horror stories. Although it lacks the controlled power of John Hersey's *Hiroshima*, it is still an extremely powerful evocation of the terror that ensued the day the bomb was dropped.

94. Endō Shūsaku. *The Sea and Poison* [Umi to Dokuyaku]. Tr. by Michael Gallagher. London: Peter Owen, 1972. 167 pp.

The narrator of *The Sea and Poison* has moved to a residential area near Tokyo to escape the hottest months of the summer. While there he meets a certain Dr. Suguro, a seedy and vaguely disreputable man. Although Dr. Suguro makes him strangely uneasy, the narrator is intrigued by this man. During World War II, Suguro, then a young doctor, had been working in a tuberculosis hospital. He was distressed by what he saw, but it was a time when life was cheap. The ill and dying inside the hospital and those outside suffering in the air raids were, it seemed, very much alike—all victims.

The second half of the book deals with the responses of a nurse whose own life has been unfulfilled, and with a particularly inhumane intern indifferent to suffering. They participate in an operation on an American POW to see how much of a man's lungs can be removed before he dies. Suguro is involved in this medical experiment, and the description of the operation graphically conveys the agony with which he must live for the rest of his life.

The novel derives its force more from the impact of the subject than from any narrative skill, and the ending suggests Suguro's guilt without giving much insight into his tortured soul.

95. Endō Shūsaku. *Silence* [Chinmoku]. Tr. by William John-
    ston. Tokyo, and Rutland, Vermont: Charles E. Tuttle Co.,
    1969. 306 pp.

Silence, like Nagayo's *The Bronze Christ* (no. 58), deals with the Jesuit missions to Japan in the seventeenth century, during the time of their repression by the Japanese government. Endō Shūsaku, himself a Christian, narrates the story of Sebastian Rodrigues, who comes to Japan with a fellow priest to minister to those Japanese converted to Christianity and to discover the truth about Christavao Ferreira, a Jesuit of impeccable courage who is said to have renounced his religion under torture.

The Japanese at first put few hindrances in the way of the first Christian missions to their country, but a number of factors, including the fear that religious conversion was an opening wedge for military invasion, led to the bloody suppression of the new religion. Against this background Rodrigues comes to Japan, excited but apprehensive. He manages to enter the country and is harbored by some villagers who have secretly retained their Christian faith.

Vague rumors are heard of Ferreira, but nothing certain. Rodrigues continues his ministry among the villagers, until one day he is betrayed by Kinchijiro, a man whose combined weakness and guilt make him very much like Judas. Rodrigues is imprisoned along with some of the villagers but continues to serve them quietly. Such an existence cannot last, however, and he and a fellow priest are asked to trample on a sacred image. If they refuse three of the villagers will be drowned in the ocean. They do refuse, and Rodrigues watches with horror as his fellow priest plunges into the ocean after the villagers and drowns himself.

Later, taken to Nagasaki, Rodrigues meets the by-now-legendary Ferreira, who explains how he could not bear the burden for the terrible sufferings of the Japanese Christians who were tortured for his refusal to renounce his faith. Rodrigues is moved by Ferreira's confession. He too has been overwhelmed by the suffering of these people while—as he says—God remained silent.

Inoue, the magistrate interrogating Rodrigues, advocates what seems to him the most sensible course—that of apostasy. After Rodrigues complies, Inoue insists that Rodrigues was defeated not by him but by "this swamp of Japan," where an alien religion like Christianity could not take root. Much of the impact of this moving and perplexing novel stems from its ambiguity—its refusal to praise or condemn Rodrigues. *Silence* is perhaps the only modern Japanese novel that has the religious depth and resonance of the works of such Western novelists as Graham Greene and Francois Mauriac.

96. Abe Kōbō. *The Woman in the Dunes* [Suna no Onna]. Tr. by E. Dale Saunders. New York: Alfred A. Knopf, 1964. 239 pp. (Paperback, Berkley Medallion Books).

A man comes to a remote seashore on a holiday to collect insects. He is a teacher, and a solitary person with no binding human ties. When he asks for lodging, the villagers take him to a house at the bottom of a large sand pit, the home of an equally solitary woman. The next morning he finds the rope ladder by which he had descended drawn up, and gradually he comes to realize that he will not be allowed to leave. In order to survive, he and the woman must spend a large portion of the day digging out the sand that continually falls about them in small avalanches. *The Woman in the Dunes* records the minute details of this life, the man's relationship with the woman, and his eventual reconciliation to his pointless, forcibly sequestered existence.

The Woman in the Dunes implies that the lot of most men is like that of the couple in the sandpit. The one time the man does make his way to the surface in an unsuccessful attempt to escape, he finds out that the life of the villagers there is hardly different from his own in the pit. The novel contains many subtle observations, but much of its effectiveness stems from its use of convincing physical detail.

97. Abe Kōbō. *The Face of Another* [Tanin no Kao]. Tr. by E. Dale Saunders. New York: Alfred A. Knopf, 1966. 237 pp.

Abe is pre-eminently the Japanese novelist of the faceless, uncertain man who comes to doubt even his own reality. A scientist who has been horribly disfigured in an explosion during an experiment narrates his story, mostly in several notebooks. Since the accident has obliterated his features, he conceives the idea of constructing another face. First he talks with a fellow scientist who has been able to develop a material very like human skin. Then he studies the whole idea of the face, consults a book (Henri Boulan's *Le Visage*) that classifies different kinds of faces, and speculates that the soul and heart "can only be negotiated through the face." Yet, he also realizes that the face conceals as much as it reveals, and is fascinated by primitive masks and those used in Noh plays. More profoundly, he begins to believe that the new face he is contriving so carefully will give him freedom—perhaps even make him into another person.

He sees that the people around him all have made their faces into masks. They serve the need for concealment as much as the masks of executioners, thieves, and priests of secret societies. His new face, he decides, is hardly different from the masked faces of others that also hide the deepest self.

He rents a room, lets it be known that his younger brother has come to live with him, and assumes that younger brother's role, wearing his new face. In this guise, posing as a different person and "possessed by frantic sexual fantasies," he sets out to seduce his own wife. He succeeds with ease but paradoxically becomes jealous of himself. One day, upon returning to his room, he discovers a farewell letter from his wife, in which she tells him she had recognized him immediately. Instead of giving him freedom, his new face, she tells him, has only led him into endless introspection, "like a snake with its tail in its mouth." In his final confession, he understands that he will always be isolated from others, lonely and full of hate. "Perhaps the act of writing is necessary only when nothing happens."

Abe's novels are all concerned with the disintegration and reestablishment of identity, but *The Face of Another* is considerably different from *The Woman in the Dunes*. That novel was anchored in the reality of the sandpit and the woman. Here only the narrator is real, and even he, for all his frank confession, is often hazily motivated. Much of the narrator's speculation seems disembodied, seldom related to specific action. But, as a novel of the lonely and dispossessed, *The Face of Another* has haunting reverberations.

98. Abe Kōbō. *The Ruined Map* [Moetsukita Chizu]. Tr. by E. Dale Saunders. New York: Alfred A. Knopf, 1969. 299 pp.

Abe's novels deal with urban man threatened with dissolution of the self. *The Ruined Map* is a puzzling book. A private detective is employed by a fascinating, enigmatic woman to find her husband, Nemuro, who had disappeared some months before. The wife's responses to the detective's questions are vague and unsettling. With skimpy evidence, the detective begins his investigations.

He encounters the wife's brother, a mysterious man who appears to know more than he reveals. The brother insists that to survive a man needs a map to provide comforting guidance in a malevolent world "full of wild beasts." Throughout his search, the detective repeatedly encounters this man, who appears to have disreputable underworld connections.

In the shadowy urban world of this novel, identities are unclear. The detective suggests to Nemuro's wife that her brother is not what he appears to be, and even hints at an illicit relationship. She denies this, suggesting that her brother is a homosexual, which the detective finds even more baffling. The detective muses that the missing man simply decided to disappear to escape the constricting persona society had cursed him with. The detective himself is attracted by such thoughts of escape.

He hears that the brother has been murdered. Soon afterward, a fellow employee of Nemuro, who has been helpful to him, commits suicide. Somehow the underworld seems involved. The detective is brutally beaten, and returns to the apartment of the mysterious woman who hired him. From this point he gradually loses the feeling of his own identity; it is an amnesia he welcomes: the dissolving sense of self which gives him a new, strange freedom.

The Ruined Map is a haunting novel of the labyrinthine modern city and the people who traverse its tortuous ways. Although neither characters nor plot are ever distinct, the haziness of the atmosphere is very real. Abe, in his earlier novels, has dissolved the identity of his protagonists, only to reestablish it in a new way. Here we see only the dissolution of the self without rehabilitation.

99.   Abe Kōbō. *Inter Ice Age 4* [Dai Yon Kampyō-ki]. Tr. by E. Dale Saunders. New York: Alfred A. Knopf, 1970. 228 pp. (Paperback, Berkley Medallion Books).

The setting of *Inter Ice Age 4* is the immediate future. Professor Katsumi, who narrates the story, is in charge of a computer that can predict the future. He and his assistant choose a man to use in their experiments, but the man dies in a manner that implicates them. Katsumi is allowed some vision into the future of humanity, and through this exploration the novel examines some of Abe's favorite themes: the deceptive, nebulous nature of the self, and the strange reality of things about man that fascinate and menace him.

In this novel, Abe's philosophical discursiveness, which since *The Face of Another* has been appropriating more and more of the narrative, reaches a new height. As one reads Abe one acquires the suspicion that the life of things takes on more meaning for Abe than the lives of people.

100.   Mishima Yukio. *Confessions of a Mask* [Kamen no Kokuhaku]. Tr. by Meredith Weatherby. New York: New Directions, 1958. 256 pp. (Paperback).

Confessions of a Mask is narrated in the first person by a young man who, from an early age, senses that he is different from other men. As a child, he was always fascinated by stories and pictures of violence and cruelty. He is obsessed by the martyrdom of St. Sebastian. A picture of that beautiful young man suffering the torments of death aroused him to his first ejaculation. A young classmate at school, Omi, excites the narrator to similar fantasies, and he takes perverse pleasure in dreams of stabbing Omi and watching the blood drip from his supple flesh. Realizing that his inner thoughts set him apart from his friends, he tries to give the appearance of sharing his schoolmates' interest in girls, but always fears that his true feelings will betray him.

Much of the story takes place during World War II, and the narrator welcomes the prospect of imminent destruction, which seems more attractive than the tedious, plodding everyday life he is convinced awaits him. He visits a friend who has enlisted in the army, and is attracted to his friend's eighteen-year-old sister, Sonoko. He kisses her but finds in himself no desire for sexual fulfillment. A mutual friend then tells him she wishes to marry him. Unable to declare his affection for her, he sends a refusal, and she marries someone else.

The war ends without the wished-for catastrophe, and the hated demands of ordinary life assert themselves. He asks a friend to take him to a prostitute, hoping to prove his masculinity, but he is impotent. He meets Sonoko again several times, perhaps as a last effort to demonstrate his sexual normality. One day at a coffeehouse the sight of a half-naked young man, muscular and handsome, distracts his attention from her, and the book concludes in a daydream in which he stabs the young man.

Confessions of a Mask is a frank, unrestrained portrait of a sadistic homosexual. Although the narrator is involved with a number of people, no one—neither family, friend, nor lover —has much reality for him. Instead, all the resources of the author are concentrated on a meticulous examination of the narrator's perverse development.

101. Mishima Yukio. *Thirst for Love* [Ai no Kawaki]. Tr. by Alfred H. Marks. New York: Alfred A. Knopf, 1966. 200 pp. (Paperback, Berkley Medallion Books).

Thirst for Love is the story of Etsuko Sugimoto, widow of a brutal, philandering husband who has come to Maidemmura, near Osaka, to live with her husband's family. She becomes her father-in-law's mistress, and later falls in love with Saburo, a young man who does farm work. Her new love is complicated by the recollected failures of her marriage and the aridity of her present incestuous relationship. The explosive denouement makes sense, though it does come as a surprise.

The greatest value of the book lies in its adroit handling of Etsuko's jealousy, first excited by her husband and later by the unsuspecting Saburo's dalliance with a servant girl. The illness and death of Etsuko's husband from typhoid fever, and the family visit to a fire-lit local shrine festival reveal Mishima's descriptive powers at their best. The associations of those scenes with the imagery of the title "thirst for love," (in Japanese, literally, "dryness of love") show well Mishima's abilities as a symbolist.

102. Mishima Yukio. *Forbidden Colors* [Kinjiki]. Tr. by Alfred H. Marks. New York: Alfred A. Knopf, 1968. 403 pp. (Paperback, Avon Books).

Forbidden Colors, written in 1954, has been acclaimed by some as Mishima's masterpiece. It is at least a highly representative Mishima work, for it contains most of the elements that distinguish his writings: elaborate plotting, lush simile and metaphor, anti-feminism, opposition to conventional morality, the extolling of male beauty, and suicide.

Forbidden Colors is the saga of the homosexual and heterosexual activities of an attractive young married man. The plot is involved primarily with the efforts of this man, Yuichi Minami, to live his own life, free of the machinations of a heterosexual and aging author, Shunsuke Hinoki, who uses Yuichi to entrap and disappoint women who have resisted his advances. The book begins with Yuichi's first meeting with Shunsuke, who is at the time romantically interested in the girl Yuichi is supposed to marry. When Yuichi confesses to Shunsuke his fear of women and his interest in men, Shunsuke advises him to marry the unsuspecting fiancée, thus making her the first victim of their conspiracy against womankind. He also buys, for a large sum of money, Yuichi's cooperation in several plots to entrap other women. The book ends with the death of Shunsuke, over a year and several broken hearts—male as well as female —later.

This work has much to say about homosexuality, particularly among men who are not suspected of such proclivities, and about an ideal of male beauty that transcends sex. A number of authors who have written on homosexuality—all the way back to Plato—are cited and their works alluded to and even imitated. The most important authors so treated are Oscar Wilde, Andre Gide, and Thomas Mann—Mann principally for his *Death in Venice*, a story of another aging heterosexual author's romantic interest in a beautiful young male. The result is a slow-moving yet erotic work, heavily larded with disquisitions by Shunsuke and the omniscient narrator, drawing attention to the human themes of the humor, the mystique, and the agonies of homosexuality, the difficulties imposed by Japanese marital conventions on all concerned, and the vagaries of human love.

103. Mishima Yukio. *The Sound of Waves* [Shiosai]. Tr. by Meredith Weatherby. New York: Alfred A. Knopf, 1956. 141 pp. (Paperback, Berkley Medallion Books).

This novel, strikingly unlike most of Mishima's fiction, deals with heterosexual love in a simple, idyllic fashion. Shinji, an eighteen-year-old fisherman, lives on an island remote from the attractions of modern civilization. He is in love with Hatsue, the daughter of a well-to-do villager. Hatsue is also attracted to Shinji, and they express their love when they meet accidentally in a deserted building near the sea. Hatsue's father, having promised his daughter to a self-important young man whose prospects are better than those of Shinji, forbids his daughter any contact with him, but withdraws his objections after Shinji distinguishes himself on a stormy fishing voyage by swimming to a buoy to secure a broken lifeline.

The Sound of Waves is notable for its portrayal of the traditional

round of life in a small Japanese village. But apart from the
act of physical valor that sets Shinji apart from others, there
is nothing uniquely characteristic of Mishima in this short novel.
It is, however, a vivid depiction of life in a Japanese fishing
village in the Inland Sea.

104. Mishima Yuko. *The Temple of the Golden Pavilion* [Kinka-
     kuji]. Tr. by Ivan Morris. Introduction by Nancy Wilson
     Ross. New York: Alfred A. Knopf, 1951. 262 pp. (Paper-
     back, Berkley Medallion Books).

Based upon an actual event, *The Temple of the Golden Pavilion*
tells of a young Buddhist acolyte of unsound mind who set
fire to and destroyed the centuries'-old Temple of the Golden
Pavilion, a national treasure in Kyoto. Mishima's novel is narrated by Mizoguchi, the young arsonist, who, in recounting
the story of his life, explains how he came to commit his horren-
dous act.

The son of a poor Zen priest, Mizoguchi harbors deep feelings
of inferiority. He is embarrassed by his father's weakness, and
is isolated from his peers because of his stutter. Mocked by
other boys for this affliction, he contrasts his own inadequacy
to the shining, impervious image of the lovely temple. He lives
an arrogant inner life of antipathy, and resentment, considering
the temple an affront to his poor existence.

When his father dies, Mizoguchi is enrolled among the acolytes. During these early years he longs for the American bombing raids to destroy the hated temple, but since Kyoto was
spared, his hope is thwarted. One of the few good experiences
of his life among the acolytes is his friendship with Tsurukawa.
But the boy's death deprives him of his last positive influence.
The friend who replaces him, Kashiwagi, is a sinister figure.
Clubfooted and cynical, he is devoid of human feeling—the
embodiment of Mizoguchi's distrust of others.

Mizoguchi's relations with the abbot are ambivalent. The
abbot is a fat, apparently worldly man, who smokes cigarettes
and has assignations with loose women. Yet his inner self is
totally hidden. Mizoguchi, who has learned from bitter experi-

ence to define his own being through contempt for others, tries to goad the abbot into rejecting him. But his carefully planned insults are met with inscrutability. In his obscure way the abbot seems to be trying to help Mizoguchi.

Mizoguchi insists that beauty is his "most deadly enemy." Yet he also realizes that the beauty of the Golden Temple is indestructible:

Nothingness was the very structure of this beauty. Therefore, from the incompletion of the various details of the beauty there arose automatically an adumbration of nothingness, and this delicate building, wrought of the most slender timber, was trembling in anticipation of nothingness, like a jeweled necklace trembling in the wind.

He decides that he "must do the deed precisely because it was so futile." He sets fire to the temple and escapes, feeling "like a man who settles down for a smoke after finishing a job of work. I wanted to live."

The Temple of the Golden Pavilion is clearly the finest Japanese novel since *The Makioka Sisters* (no. 54). From one vantage point Mizoguchi's act can be seen as a brilliant fulfillment of Buddhist teaching, a Zen *acte gratuite*. Another perspective shows him engaged in a perverse, destructive affirmation of self in the manner of other Mishima heroes. Beautifully translated, this novel, subtle and reverberative, more searching than *Confessions of a Mask* and more concentrated than *Forbidden Colors*, is likely to rank as Mishima's masterpiece.

105. Mishima Yukio. *After the Banquet* [Utage no Ato]. Tr. by Donald Keene. New York: Alfred A. Knopf, 1963. 270 pp. (Paperback, Berkley Medallion Books).

Kazu, a woman of fifty, is still beautiful, and the owner of a successful Tokyo restaurant, The Setsugoan, patronized by influential members of the Conservative Party. One evening she is hostess to a group of aging politicians of the Radical Party. One of them dies suddenly, sounding the theme of old age which permeates the novel. Noguchi, who is present, impresses Kazu with his quiet, assured bearing. The two meet a number of times and decide to marry. Kazu is attracted by the prospect of having her ashes rest with a man of distinguished family. Also appealing to her is the idea of rescuing this fine old man from his genteel poverty.

) Each seems to bring to their union what was lacking in the other. Kazu is a creature of "warm blood and . . . human vitality," while Noguchi embodies "lofty ideals and beautiful principles." When the Radical Party chooses Noguchi to run as their candidate for mayor of Tokyo, he accepts, and Kazu backs him to the full. She uses the money carefully saved for her old age and speaks effectively and successfully on his behalf. An enemy, however, circulates a scandalous account of her life, reducing her husband's vote enough to allow the conservative nominee to win.

Noguchi, however, is content to retire with his wife on their modest income. But the restless Kazu goes to her old conservative patrons to obtain pledge money for the reopening of The Setsugoan restaurant. Her husband and his friends consider this a betrayal, and Noguchi asks for a divorce, which Kazu willingly grants.

After the Banquet is neither the best nor the worst of Mishima's novels. Its objectivity is far removed from the obsessive quality of his best works (*The Temple of the Golden Pavilion* and *Confessions of a Mask*), but the portrayal of the conflict of two opposing personalities is straightforward and effective.

106. Mishima Yukio. *The Sailor Who Fell from Grace with the Sea* [Gogo no Eikō]. Tr. by John Nathan. New York: Alfred A. Knopf, 1965. 181 pp. (Paperback, Berkley Medallion Books).

Noboru, a thirteen-year-old boy, experiences an almost religious experience when he watches, through a small peephole, his widowed mother in bed with her lover, a sailor named Ryuji. Noboru belongs to a gang of boys on the verge of adolescence who "fill the world's great hollows" through such acts as the killing and dissection of a kitten. Despising the weak and ordinary, they ruthlessly search to achieve "real power over existence."

Noboru's mother, Fusako, is a successful thirty-three-year-old businesswoman, who has no idea of her son's predilections. Her sailor lover is intensely admired by Noboru because of his association with the primal reality of the sea. Ryuji had always loved freedom and resisted any sort of domestic cares, but now, attracted by a more stable life, he proposes marriage to Fusako. After some hesitation, she accepts. This leads Noboru and his gang to despise Ryuji, who is giving up the challenging heroism of a sailor's life for the ordinary routine of everyday existence.

Instead of remaining a sailor, Ryuji will become husband and father. And the gang hates fathers, "the flies of this world." The leader of the gang decides to kill and dissect Ryuji, as they did the kitten, to save his heroism: "the world is empty and . . . the important thing, the only thing, is to try to maintain order in that emptiness."

This short novel, told with fine economy and suspense, is a beautiful statement of Mishima's philosophy of the perverse, existential act. Harrowing and at times unbearably direct, it recalls *The Stranger* by Camus in its insistence that only man's actions can fabricate the reality of his world. The translation is excellent. The title, far from a direct translation of the Japanese—literally, "Launching in the Afternoon"—was, according to John Nathan, suggested by Mishima himself.

107. Mishima Yukio. *Sun and Steel* [Taiyō to Tetsu]. Tr. by John Bester. Tokyo: Kodansha International, 1970. 104 pp. (Paperback, Grove Press).

This long essay was first published in Japanese in 1968, and appeared in translation in America a few months before Mishima's suicide. Mishima, in this work, throws off the elaborate disguises of the purveyor of fiction. He writes candidly of his conversion from the world of "Novalis's night and Yeatsian Irish twilights" to the world of the sun, which tanned his skin and brought him to value muscle, the sword, the rifle, the jet plane, and violent death.

The book is absolutely essential to one who wishes to understand Mishima's bizarre death by harakiri and ritual beheading. It is the best rendition in English of Mishima's philosophical style.

108. Mishima Yukio. *Spring Snow* [Haru no Yuki]. *The Sea of Fertility*, vol. 1. Tr. by Michael Gallagher. New York: Alfred A. Knopf, 1972. 336 pp.

On November 25, 1970, Mishima Yukio committed ritual suicide. That morning he had completed the fourth volume of his tetralogy *The Sea of Fertility*, of which *Spring Snow* is the initial volume. Over a number of years Mishima had prepared himself, in his works, for his suicide, leaving instructions for the publication in English of all four volumes of *The Sea of Fertility*.

Spring Snow, though it answers for us some of the larger riddles of Mishima's writings, is essentially a delicate, sad love story. Two young lovers have an affair that sputters uncertainly until the girl is engaged to a grandson of the emperor, at which time it flames out with the fury of "distant fire." The intensity of the affair, combined with the knowledge of both lovers of its futility, evokes what Mishima called the "sick romanticism" of the German romantic writers he loved and identified with, as well as the love-suicide plots of so many Kabuki and Japanese puppet theater plays.

Behind the love story moves the reality of a changing Japan. The Emperor Meiji, who altered Japan so vastly beginning in 1867, has died. In 1912 his son, the Emperor Taishō, is taking over. It is a new era, and in memory of the old era a picture of an assembled mass of young Japanese soldiers who died in the Russo-Japanese war recurs in the mind of young Kiyoaki Matsugae, the protagonist of the novel.

There is more than a hint here of the World War II of Mishima's first important work, *Confessions of a Mask*, which tells the reader so much about how the memory of the dead of an earlier war might have affected Mishima, filling him with a sense of indebtedness that only his own heroic quasi-military death would redeem.

At one point in *Spring Snow* Kiyoaki discusses with his friend Honda, a law student, how the times are changing. Honda says, "The age of glorious wars ended with the Meiji era.... There isn't much chance now to die on the battlefield.... But now that the old wars are finished, a new kind of war has just begun; this is the era of the war of emotion.... And just as in the old wars, there will be casualties in the war of emotion, I think. It's the fate of our age—and you're one of our representatives. So what about it then? You're fully resolved to die in this new war—am I right?"

Again, transparently, Kiyoaki's Meiji-era war is Mishima's World War II. And can it be that Mishima saw our time as one in which a heroic young man can distinguish himself not so much by death on the battlefield as by public self-immolation? Did Mishima see a connection between himself and Jan Palach? The public martyr?

Most importantly, Mishima works to develop in *Spring Snow* a novel that has broader implications than those of the Japan of 1912. The family of the protagonist is cosmopolitan, international. They show films at their parties, have a friend with a Rolls-Royce, and attempt at one point to send their lovesick son to Oxford. They have as houseguests for a time two Siamese princes studying at Kiyoaki's school. The Siamese princes carry the story beyond the Japanese East to the East of southeast Asia, and introduce doctrines of metempsychosis that go beyond those normally available to young Kiyoaki. The novel thus develops a world-view and a philosophy that transcends the common East-West dialectic of Japanese novels.

The metempsychosis preoccupation permits unification of the tetralogy through characters living different incarnations of the same souls in the various novels. Through its use of metempsychosis, this novel illustrates Mishima's complex answer to the malaise of modernity he felt he suffered, an answer Western thought and its Aristotelian logic, Mishima felt, were unable to arrive at: the idea that man makes his own heaven and his own hell in a world in which transmigration is constantly taking

place, in which man must, like Kiyoaki, "open his soul to the
four great inchoate elements of fire, wind, water and earth. . . . "

The book is well constructed, with a compelling story line
and the similes and metaphors that Mishima handled with such
grace. Michael Gallagher treats these with great sensitivity.

109. Mishima Yukio. *Runaway Horses* [Homba]. *The Sea of
Fertility*, vol. 2. Tr. by Michael Gallagher. New York: Alfred
A. Knopf, 1973. 421 pp.

Runaway Horses is the story of young Isao Iinuma, the
Buddhist reincarnation of Kiyoaki Matsugae, hero of *Spring
Snow*. The period of Isao's life recounted, however, is con-
ditioned not so much by Buddhist as by Shintō considerations,
showing the relationships among emperor worship, assassination politics, harakiri, and Shintō liturgy. Much of the action
is viewed by Shigekuni Honda, an important character of *Spring
Snow*, now a respected judge, whose faith in law and the objec-
tive realities in which it is rooted is gradually undermined by
his discovery of Isao's uncanny physical and psychical affinities
with the long-dead Kiyoaki, and by his tardy recognition of
realities that go beyond the grave, realities constantly at work
in the present moment.

Runaway Horses takes place twenty years after the events of
Spring Snow, in 1932. Unemployment and economic ills, particularly in the farming communities, are inciting strong anti-
capitalist cabals against the government, from both the Left and
the Right. The greatest vigilance is exerted against communists, who are frequently imprisoned and tortured by the police
agencies. Rightist rebels, loyal to the emperor and frequently
backed by an army drawing its recruits from destitute farmers,
lash out with bursts of assassinations, followed by harakiri for
some of the perpetrators and judicial leniency for others.

Runaway Horses thus provides Mishima with an opportunity
to present his own death to come in a political context, with
certain similarities to that of his own time. Its hero, Isao Iinuma,
has rejected the ideology of the political Left, even while admiring the dedication of its adherents. The small force he dominates,

as Mishima dominated his Shield Society, has the monarchistic leanings of Mishima's force, as well as a speaking acquaintance with the military Mishima enjoyed, and which he used to stage his death.

Isao also has available the choice between a soul-denying Buddhism and a transcendentally pantheistic Shintoism (Mishima before his death renounced Buddhism in favor of Shintoism). He fights for principle in a world without principle, in which his death for a cause will be admired only for its beauty, never for what it accomplishes. He is fighting, in the end, for a Japanese ideal which many may have forgotten, but which his death will forcibly revivify. Yet, he is betrayed, as so many Mishima heroes are betrayed, by a woman who thinks she loves him but really wants, like Stendhal's Mathilde, in *The Red and the Black*, only a vicarious share in his martyrdom.

110. Nozaki Akiyuki. *The Pornographers* [Erogotoshi-tachi]. Tr. by Michael Gallagher. New York: Alfred A. Knopf, 1968. 304 pp. (Paperback, Bantam Books).

In this novel Subuyan (whose name means "pickled pork") sees his mother die in an incendiary raid during World War II, and the memory of her burnt flesh haunts him. He is an enterprising man married to an older woman, Oharu, who has a teen-age daughter, Keiko. Subuyan is an ordinary man in every respect except his profession: he is a pornographer. He is in the business of renting and selling "blue" movies with his partner Banteki. Although he branches out into other areas of his "profession," including the actual making of the films and the furnishing of fake virgins to eager customers, he is discontented with the general quality of pornographic movies. Subuyan and Banteki, with the assistance of a writer of "dirty" books, plan to produce films that are more artistic. The technical difficulties of making such movies are comically contrasted with the emotions the films are meant to arouse. The whole business of pandering to the repressed desires of members of the so-called respectable middle class is described in *The Pornographer* with irony and a touch of compassion.

Subuyan is distracted temporarily from his business when Oharu becomes pregnant. They decide on an abortion, and Oharu dies, leaving Subuyan stepfather to Keiko, now a young woman. Subuyan is sexually attracted to her, and Keiko responds to his advances. But he finds he is impotent. She disappears, and throughout the remainder of the novel he searches for her, feeling sure that she is the only cure for his impotence.

Subuyan is arrested but escapes with a fine and resolves to organize his profession in such a way that he will be less vulnerable to the law. He brings together a group of prostitutes, continues to make pornographic movies, and organizes orgies. He insists that money alone is not his motivation: "The reason I'm in this business is because of the sadness of the human condition—especially men." In a way, he even thinks of himself as a priest ministering to the neglected, darker side of life. He seeks justification in the orgies, so carefully arranged, but is only saddened by them. During one, he goes out, is struck by a car, and is killed. Only in Subuyan's death does Keiko find him again, discovering that he has recovered in his death that which he has lost in life.

The Pornographers is not a pornographic novel. Achieving exactly the right measure of comedy and sadness, its strange cast of characters has no villains. The pathos of a group of people who purvey illusion to those whose lives are unfulfilled is conveyed, demonstrating how the pornographer may himself be robbed of the illusion he sells to the public he panders to.

111. Ishihara Shintarō. *Season of Violence* [Taiyō no Kisetsu]. Tr. by John G. Mills, Takahama Toshie, and Ken Tremayne. Rutland, Vermont, and Tokyo: Charles E. Tuttle Co., 1966. 153 pp.

These three novellas, "Season of Violence," "The Punishment Room," and "The Yacht and the Boy," are all clinical portrayals of young men in postwar Japan for whom the reader is likely to feel little or no sympathy.

"Season of Violence" had great influence among young Japanese men when it was published in 1956. All relationships in this story are based on competition. Tatsuya, the protagonist, is intensely proud of his ability as a boxer. There is no true friendship in his association with his comrades, no element of self-sacrifice in their relationships. Instead, a carefully balanced system of debit and credit is at work. If the debit column grows too long, the friendship breaks up.

Women are seen only as adversaries to be overcome and subdued. Tatsuya meets his match in Eiko, who is "determined to take from men and give nothing in return." Their relationship, starting as only another of the contests by which people prove themselves, proves to be deeply felt. Eiko becomes pregnant. Tatsuya insists that she have an abortion, and she dies. "Her death was the supreme challenge. He had lost his favorite toy, the toy he could never break no matter how much he battered it."

"The Punishment Room" (Shokei no Heya) is a luridly detailed description of a beating given an adolescent by those he has betrayed.

The final story, "The Yacht and the Boy," (Yotto no Shōnen) is equally sadistic. The main character, the "boy" as he is called through most of the story, works on the yacht of a wealthy American and has an intense desire for a small yacht of his own. He threatens others physically, and carefully adds to his savings by extorting money from them. Finally, with help from the American, he is able to realize his dream. Later, when acquaintances mock him for his relationship with a prostitute, he sabotages their boat and unintentionally kills his only friend. In despair, the boy sails his hard-won yacht onto dangerous rocks, and he is drowned.

Neither subtle nor technically proficient, these three stories make no claim to profundity, but possess a crude power and uncompromising clarity. The author makes no appeal to the reader's sympathy in behalf of his characters. Ishihara does not equal Genet's philosophical justification for evil. He presents the world as he sees it with shocking honesty, offering no explanations and demanding no sentimental response.

112. Ōe Kenzaburō. *A Personal Matter* [Kojinteki na Taiken]. Tr. by John Nathan. New York: Grove Press, 1969. 214 pp. (Paperback).

Ōe is a spokesman for the youth in Japan, and himself the youngest of the novelists whose works appear in this *Guide*. *A Personal Matter* was published in Japan in 1965 and is clearly influenced by the Western existentialist novel. The protagonist —called Bird—is a married but aimless man in his early twenties. "It seemed to him now, looking back on those terrible days, that with the exception of listening to music and drinking and immersing in harsh, drunken sleep, he hadn't engaged in a single living human activity. . . . He was like a mental incompetent with only the slightest chance of recovery, but he had to tame all over again not only the wilderness inside himself, but the wilderness of his relations to the world outside." Bird reads widely in the literature of Europe and America of the last hundred years and finds again and again, to his dismay, his own alienated self.

When his wife gives birth to a baby with a brain hernia, the child seems to Bird a hideous confirmation of his own inner deformity, of the horror he sees in the world about him. He begins a desperate affair with Himiko, a promiscuous woman whose husband has committed suicide.

Repeated visits to the hospital—his revulsion at his child's oversized head and the antiseptic unconcern of the medical officials at the hospital—depress him even more. He resolves, with Himiko's advice, to take the child to a clinic where it will be allowed to die quietly, but at the last moment changes his mind and returns with the child to his family.

A Personal Matter is rich with clinical detail, and the two major characters, Bird and Himiko, are sharply defined. The non-Japanese reader may feel, however, that much of the anguish and despair are tiredly derived from modern Western literature about the alienated man. The positive ending is abrupt and too rapidly motivated.

113. Japan Writers' Society. *Young Forever and Five Other Novelettes by Contemporary Japanese Authors.* Tokyo: Hokuseido Press, 1941. 142 pp.

The six short works of fiction that make up this volume are

of varying quality. *Young Forever* (by Yokomitsu Riichi, translated by Kodama Habuku) tells of a successful businessman who retires, after reaching the pinnacle of his career, only to return confidently to assert himself once more as the outstanding member of his profession. *Starry Night* (by Abe Tomoji, translated by Hisakazu Kaneko) is the story of two young genealogists employed by a wealthy nobleman to research his family history. *He Who Inherits* (by Wada Den, translated by Kunitomo Tado) portrays an aging son who suffers impatiently his peasant father's unwillingness to relinquish any portion of the family assets. The recurrent theme of these three stories—the best of the collection—is the secure and confident dominance of the older, traditional generation over the younger. It is clear in all these stories that rebellion is futile and the young can only submit and obey. The other stories in this volume are *The G.S.L. Club* by Fukada Kyuya, *A Rich Poor Father* by Serizawa Mitsujiro, and *Shopgirl* by Uno Chiyo.

The stories, issued by the Japan Writers' Society, present a lucid if not particularly profound view of Japanese society on the eve of World War II, but the translations are generally marred by awkward and often ungrammatical English.

114. Keene, Donald, ed. *Modern Japanese Literature*. New York: Grove Press, 1956. 440 pp. (Paperback).

This, the second volume of the monumental Donald Keene anthology, is not only a fine introduction to Japanese literature since 1868 but also a compendium of twentieth-century Japanese prose. It includes short stories, passages from novels, modern *haiku* and *waka*, a scene from a *kabuki* play, a modern play that is a delightfully complex commentary on the possession theme so common in early Japanese literature, a passage from the important critical work *The Essence of the Novel*, some translations from modern poetry in both Chinese and Japanese, and two prose relics from the newly Westernized Japan—"The Beefeater" and "The Western Peep Show."

Two novelettes of exceptional merit in the anthology are "Growing up," by Higuchi Ichiyō, and "The Sumida River," by Nagai Kafū. "Growing Up" traces a group of children coming of age in the Yoshiwara, Tokyo's red-light district. "The Sumida River" depicts a boy and girl growing up in better surroundings but still caught by the demands of family, society, and their own desires.

Also included are two haunting selections by Akutagawa Ryūnosuke, author of "Rashōmon"; a famous moral enigma entitled "Han's Crime," by Shiga Naoya; the riddling, ghostly "Tale of Three Who Were Blind," by Izumi Kyōka; "Villon's Wife," by Dazai Osamu; and the passage "Omi," from Mishima's *Confessions of a Mask*. There are two excellent selections by Tanizaki Junichirō, one a passage from *The Makioka Sisters*, and the other a rather ghastly piece titled "The Mother of Captain Shigemoto." Kawabata Yasunari, Japan's only winner of the Nobel Prize for Literature, is represented by a subtle psychological story, "The Mole."

This volume is even more valuable because it includes important works not accessible in translation elsewhere. Some of the sad life of Ishikawa Takuboku is seen in his *Romaji Diary*. "Time," by Yokomitsu Riichi, is a somewhat traditional tale of a group of penniless actors who avoid paying a hotel bill. The allegory and symbolism, however, are modern and Western. Kume Masao's *The Tiger*, finally, is a penetrating study of a modern actor's frustrations over the narrowness of his dramatic specialty—the portrayal of animal roles—and his embarrassment at seeing that the son he dotes on perceives his frustrations.

The translations are, like those of the first volume of the Keene anthology (no. 27), excellent. These two volumes testify to the extraordinary literary gifts of Donald Keene and the tremendous influence he has exerted on the development of Japanese literature as a force in the West.

115. McKinnon, Richard N., ed. *The Heart is Alone: A Selection of 20th-Century Japanese Short Stories*. Tokyo: Hokuseido Press, 1957. 171 pp.

This collection of short stories by well-known Japanese authors, including work by Kunikida Doppo and Shiga Naoya (sparsely represented in English translation), are joined by no common theme.

Akutagawa's "Flatcar" is an account of a young boy's terror when he jumps on a railroad flatcar. His "A Clod of Earth" (see no. **63**) is included. "A Soldier," by Tayama Katai, is the well-known story of the horrors of battle experienced by a soldier in the Russo-Japanese war. "Takasebune," like many of Mori Ōgai's stories, takes place in the past—in this particular story the Tokugawa era—and points out the thin line that separates a prisoner being transported for murder from his warder. "Meat and Potatoes," by Kunikida Doppo, is the longest story in the collection, and is a debate among several men about the relative merits of the hard realities of life (meat) as compared with the ideal (potatoes). In "The Patron Saint," by Shiga Naoya, a man buys a boy a delicacy he has always wanted. The man is then strangely depressed by his good deed, while the boy thinks of him as a benefactor, a saint. "Judas' Explanation," by Mushakōji Saneatsu, is a first-person narrative in which Judas justifies his betrayal of Christ. The potential ironies of this sketch are weakened, however, by the sketch following it, Mushakōji's "John, on hearing Judas' Explanation." "Spring Came on a Horse-Drawn Cart," by Yokomitsu Riichi, is an autobiographical account of a husband nursing his wife on her deathbed. "One Night," by Hirotsu Kazuo, is a short sketch about an encounter with a millipede.

These stories are characterized by irony, but in most cases the irony is tame and shallow. "A Soldier" and "A Clod of Earth" are available in other collections. The most valuable contribution of this anthology is its presentation of biographical information concerning the authors, not readily available in English.

116. Keene, Donald, tr. *The Old Woman, the Wife, and the Archer: Three Modern Japanese Short Novels.* New York: Viking Press, 1961. 172 pp.

The three novels that make up this anthology are identified

in the volume's title by the salient characteristic of the principal character of each. The first two novels have in common the theme of selfless sacrifice for another. *The Songs of Oak Mountain*, by Fukasawa Shichirō, is concerned with the legendary custom of abandoning aged people on Oak Mountain when they reach the age of seventy. Orin is pleased to see her widowed son remarry and looks forward to the time when she may go to the mountain to die and no longer be a burden on her family. The village in which she has lived for fifty years is always short of food, and each winter brings the worry of whether or not the villagers can stretch their food supply through the long cold months. Orin prepares carefully for her final journey and joyously serves the feast at the time of her departure. She leaves, accompanied by her son Tatsuhei, and peacefully sits down upon her arrival to accept her fate. Another old person, Matayan, makes the same journey but tries to return and is killed by his son.

Ohan, by Uno Chiyo, describes another selfless woman. Ohan's husband, who narrates the story, has left his wife to live with a richer woman, but he longs to return to her and his son Satoru. The husband manages a small shop and daily sees his son, who thinks he has no father. Affection between the two grows, and the husband resolves to return. Just as he is about to be reunited with Ohan, the son is accidentally killed in a great storm. At the story's end, Ohan moves away and the husband is revealed as a weak man, overwhelmed by recrimination and guilt.

The final and most ambiguous novel, *Asters*, by Ishikawa Jun, is set in medieval times and is concerned with perverse self-expression. Muneyori, having defied his father, is sent away to become governor of a remote province—a post that carries little responsibility. He learns to enjoy hunting and becomes a skilled archer. Formerly, he had enjoyed composing poetry, but now he becomes intoxicated by the "poetry" of killing. He begins to kill men, first one of his wife's lovers, then a host of people—anyone accused of however small a crime. On a strange journey to a forbidden place over the mountain he meets a mysterious man named Heita, and he returns with his bow to shoot at the figure of Buddha carved on the side of the mountain. He lets his arrow fly, and the cliff crumbles beneath him, plummeting him to his death.

All three stories are characterized by a skillful economy of narration in strong contrast to their portrayal of extremes of behavior. They all have something parabolic about them, and seem to imply that truth can only be found when human nature is expressed at extremes of behavior. Donald Keene has so skillfully rendered them into English that each appears to have, even in translation, its own unique style.

117. Seidensticker, E. G.; Bester, John; and Morris, Ivan, trs. *Modern Japanese Short Stories*. Tokyo: Japan Publications Trading Co., 1961. 286 pp.

The stories in this collection are united by the themes of loneliness, isolation, and misunderstanding. "Han's Crime," by Shiga Naoya (a writer too little translated) introduces a knife-thrower and the difficult question of whether he killed his wife deliberately or accidentally. "Osan" is another of Dazai Osamu's stories of degradation. Several other stories deal with men and women who once loved one another and whose passion has been transformed by time and circumstance into hostility, indifference, or simply solicitude. "A Bell in Fukagawa," by Kawaguchi Matsutarō, tells of a young writer who lives for a time with a woman of doubtful reputation who nonetheless loves and supports him. "The Thin Rooster," by Ozaki Kazuo, "Enchantress," by Enchi Fumiko, and "Late Chrysanthemum," by Hayashi Fumiko, are all concerned with glowing embers of emotion that are momentarily kindled by unexpected events.

"The Misshapen Ones," by Takeda Taijun, is a powerful story of a novice in a Buddhist monastery who finds it impossible to restrain the demands of the flesh. "The Azaleas of Hira," by Inoue Yasushi, is the first-person narrative of an aged scientist who has completely neglected his emotional responsibilities to his family in pursuit of his research and yet is unable to understand why his life is a failure. In *The Black Kimono* Koda Aya tells of a woman who measures the process of aging by attending funerals.

The collection also includes "The Wild Beast," by Nakajima Ton, "The Mole," by Kawabata, and "Death in Midsummer," by Mishima, all described elsewhere.

It is unfortunate that this book, published in Japan, is not more widely available in the West, for it is one of the finest collections of modern Japanese short stories ever assembled. All the stories are of extremely high quality.

118. Morris, Ivan, ed. *Modern Japanese Stories: An Anthology.* Tr. by Edward Seidensticker, George Saito, Geoffrey Sargent, and Ivan Morris. Woodcuts by Masakazu Kuwata. Rutland, Vermont, and Tokyo: Charles E. Tuttle Co., 1962. 512 pp.

This is the largest collection of Japanese modern short stories available in one volume, and the selections are uniformly of high quality. The collection has obviously been brought together in an attempt to represent most of the significant writers of modern Japanese fiction and approximate the historical development of fiction in the twentieth century.

Mishima ("The Priest and his Love"), Akutagawa ("Autumn Mountain"), Kawabata ("The Moon on the Water"), Nagai Kafū ("Hydrangea"), and Tanizaki ("Tattoo") are represented. Niwa Fumio, in "The Hateful Age," shows something of the terrible burden of caring for a conventionally venerated grandparent. Kikuchi Kan's "On the Conduct of Lord Tadano" explores the mind of a man who discovers that because of the deference shown him as a nobleman, he can never be sure of anyone's true feelings about him. "Letter Found in a Cement-Barrel," by Hayama Yoshiki, is a proletarian story expressing the sufferings of a worker.

The difficulty of establishing meaningful communication among people is the theme of a number of the stories. Most notable are Yokomitsu Riichi's "Machine" and the excerpt from Inoue's novel *The Hunting Gun*, here called "The Shotgun." Dazai Osamu's sardonic story "The Courtesy Call" deals with a boorish neighbor who tyrannizes a couple he visits.

A number of the stories present life as an almost unrelieved, awful burden. Sakaguchi Ango's "The Idiot," which takes place in Tokyo during the firebombing raids, depicts a man who reluctantly comes to envy a moronic woman because her ignorance spares her from much of what he must suffer. Hayashi Fumiko's "Downtown" is also about war's horror, and Hirabayashi's "A Man's Life" describes a prisoner who lives in nightly fear that his cellmate will kill him. There are also short sketches of varying impact by Mori Ōgai ("Under Reconstruction"), Satomi Ton ("The Camellia"), Ogawa Mimei ("The Handstand"), and Sato Haruo ("The House of the Spanish Dog").

The twenty-five stories by twenty-five authors in this collection, published between the years 1910 and 1954, are broad and varied in their impact. The quality of the translation is generally most impressive. This is surely a fundamental work for any library. An informative literary and historical introduction by Ivan Morris, notes on the authors, and a selected bibliography accompany the translations.

119. Gluck, Jay, ed. *Ukiyo: Stories of "the Floating World" of Postwar Japan*. Written and tr. by several hands. New York: Vanguard Press, 1963, 255 pp.

This collection of stories, sketches, and personal recollections is important primarily because it portrays Japanese life after World War II. All the selections have in common the sense of uncertainty that comes when traditional values break down.

Cashiered officers, soldiers of fortune, black marketeers, reluctant prostitutes, and camp followers share these pages with ordinary citizens who are uprooted and confounded by the changes brought about by the war. Taguchi Shu testifies in "Three Unforgettable Letters" to the depth of human feeling that overcomes the antagonism of countries at war, while Tsuji Masanobu depicts a continuing enmity that cannot be assuaged by a peace treaty.

The most memorable stories are "Black Market Blues," by Koh Haruto, an account of a man whose unlucky machinations in currency manipulation cause him to find more socially accept-

able work; "One World," by Serizawa Kojiro, a portrait of the
wife of a missing naval officer who is sure her husband will
someday return from the war, and who looks with dismay on
her children's rejection of the hallowed values of prewar Japan;
"A Crane that Cannot Come Back," by Seto Nanako, the diary
of a woman dying in a hospital while desperately buoyed up
by the false promise of recovery; and "The Only One," by
Nakamoto Takako, the sad story of a young woman who feels
herself degraded as the mistress of an American soldier.

These stories, in dealing with postwar Japanese life, offer
such a variety of plot and outlook, that their total impact on
the reader is considerable. The value of this volume is essentially
sociological and only secondarily literary. Undoubtedly, it offers
the most comprehensive insights into postwar Japanese society
available in English.

120. Saeki Shoichi, ed. *The Shadow of Sunrise: Selected Stories
of Japan and the War.* Tokyo, and Palo Alto, California:
Kodansha International, 1966. 186 pp.

This collection of stories of the war has no battlefield scenes.
Instead, like John Horne Burns's *The Gallery*, it deals with people on the periphery of World War II but profoundly affected
by it.

"The Catch," by Ōe Kenzaburō (translated by John Bester),
is unquestionably the best story. Set in a small Japanese village,
it is narrated by a young boy who describes what happens
when a black American flyer is captured and imprisoned in
his father's house. At first the flyer appears to the boy as a
great odoriferous dark beast, some fettered circus animal, exotic
but dangerous. Gradually a new relationship, born of curiosity
and humanity, develops between the prisoner and the boy,
and the huge black man, although never entirely humanized
in the eyes of the villagers, is free to wander about and perform
odd jobs. Then word comes to the village that the prisoner
is to be taken to higher authorities. The captive misunderstands,
is frightened, and seizes the boy as a hostage. The boy's father
takes an ax and kills the Negro, wounding his son in the process,

and in the end the villagers are left with the huge, festering corpse to bury.

The title of the story by Umezaki Haruo, "Sakurajima" (translated by D. E. Mills), is the location of a suicide battalion in the south of Japan. The narrator, Petty Officer Murakami, waits dispiritedly for the American invasion while dodging the American planes that strafe the base. The mood is one of utter hopelessness, hardly relieved by the emperor's broadcast at the end announcing the Japanese surrender. "Summer Flower," by Hara Tamiki (translated by George Saito), is another graphic account of the atomic holocaust, laconically horrifying in its detail.

"Bones" (translated by Ted T. Takaya) by the well-known novelist Hayashi Fumiko (*The Floating Cloud*, no **82**), chronicles the degradation of a Japanese wife who receives an empty bone box, without even the ashes of her dead soldier husband, and turns to prostitution to support herself.

Ibuse Masuji's "The Far-Worshiping Commander" (translated by Glenn Shaw), has some of the ironies of his *Black Rain* (no. **71**). The commander, disciplining one of his charges on a truck, falls off along with the object of his anger when the driver suddenly starts up. The soldier is killed and the commander, the very embodiment of unthinking militarism, is affected mentally. Although the war has long been over, the commander is "possessed of the hallucination that the war is still going on and the mistaken idea that he is the military man he used to be." He is, in other words, a remnant of the old military Japan surviving absurdly in a very different age.

The stories in this volume are generally descriptive and realistic, more important perhaps for their graphic representation of the horror of war than for their profound implication. Ōe's "The Catch," however, has deeper resonances and is one of the best stories on the postwar years to be represented in translation. On the whole the translations are readable and accurate.

121. Mishima Yukio and Bownas, Geoffrey, eds. *New Writing in Japan.* Paperbound. London: Penguin Books, 1972. 249 pp.

This anthology is a collection of recent stories and poems by the most recent generation of Japanese writers. It includes work by figures fairly well known in the West, such as Abe Kōbō, Ōe Kenzaburō, Ishihara Shintarō, and of course Mishima himself. Most of the selections have not appeared elsewhere. Mishima's introduction makes no attempt to give an account of Japanese literature in recent years but does offer some helpful comments on the writers included. The stories themselves are strikingly similar in technique and attitude to the most important American and European fiction of the last twenty-five years. Some stories, like those of Ishihara, Mishima, and Ōe, are intensely realistic studies of human response to war and military life. Mishima's "Patriotism" and "Death in Midsummer" are worth reading several times, while Ōe's "The Catch," (about the capture of an American airman) is one of the best stories of World War II in any language.

In Abe's "Stick," a man is transformed into a piece of wood. Haniya's "Cosmic Mirror" explores the deviousness of mental reflection, and Akiyama's "The Simple Life" is a strange meditation on loneliness.

Two other stories, more traditional in form, are about the ambiguity of love. Yoshiyuki's "Sudden Shower" deals with a man who tries to understand his affection for a prostitute, and Yasuoka's "The Pawnbroker's Wife" examines a similar situation.

Of the contributions in this volume only "Patriotism" and perhaps "The Catch" can be called great, but this collection uniquely shows the coming of an age of Japanese fiction as a genre intimately related to the universal modern experience.

NOTE TO FINDERS

The most active publishers of Japanese prose in English translation are Alfred A. Knopf of New York and Charles E. Tuttle of Rutland, Vermont, and Tokyo. Their books are available for many years. Knopf hard-cover editions often appear as Berkley Medallion paperbacks a few years after publication. They are also reprinted by English firms for sale in that country and by Tuttle for sale in Japan. Tuttle keeps its books—original editions and a wide selection of reprints—almost perpetually in stock, and the reader can easily obtain from Tuttle its catalogs of books available for purchase in the United States. University presses frequently keep books in stock for years; so do Japanese publishers, who will at times bring out a new edition decades after the last has been exhausted. A number of bookstores in the United States specialize in Asian books, new and second-hand, and some titles are to be found in Japanese import stores, which have been opening up in cities all over America in recent years. By ordering from these bookstores or the publishers listed in the entries, or securing the assistance of one or more libraries with good collections of Japanese literature in English and influential interlibrary loan departments, the reader can acquire all the books reviewed in the *Guide*.

INDEX

Authors, editors, translators, and titles given in each numbered entry are all presented below in a single alphabetic listing. Please note that the usefulness of this index is limited: persons and titles referred to in the body of the annotations and in the introduction are not indexed. An effort has been made, however, to provide a more comprehensive listing for the pre-Meiji section where several major works are frequently gathered in a single volume. Since this bibliography is arranged chronologically, the incompleteness of the index, the general editor hopes, is justifiable.

147